# Still Room for Humans

# Still Room for Humans

## *Career Planning in an AI World*

Stan Schatt, PhD

BUSINESS EXPERT PRESS

*Leader in applied, concise business books*

*For Jane, once again and always*

# Description

**Don't Let Artificial Intelligence and Robots Steal Your Job!**

*Still Room for Humans* is the only survival guide you need to stay employable in the future. This book will teach you how to:

- make yourself indispensable to your company,
- develop *soft skills* that robots and AI cannot match,
- collaborate with robots,
- retool your skills without going back to school.

You will also learn which traditionally *safe careers* and entire industries will no longer be safe in the future because of artificial intelligence. The author details why the changes caused by disruptive technology will be far greater and take place far faster than in previous industrial revolutions.

This book offers several ways to cope with the introduction of artificial intelligence and robotics to a company or organization as well as how to take advantage of the disruption likely to result from other new technologies, including 3D printing, the Internet of Things, virtual reality, green technologies, Big Data, blockchain, and nanotechnology.

*Still Room for Humans* spells out the types of jobs long associated with well-paying careers that should be avoided because they are most likely to be eliminated by artificial intelligence. It lists several new jobs that don't exist yet but will be created shortly as new technologies become more prevalent.

**Schatt provides career planning information as well as specific advice for those readers already employed.**

# Keywords

artificial intelligence; robots; automation; career planning; virtual reality; green technologies; fusion; blockchain; Internet of things; universal basic income; nanotechnology; quantum computing

# Contents

# Testimonials

*"If you are at the beginning or even middle of your career, you need to know what is coming to maximize your job satisfaction, employment potential, and income. Doing that today is problematic, given the changes to human augmentation, AI, robotics, currency, and even more disruptive technologies like nanotechnology, green tech, and quantum computing. In his book* Still Room for Humans: Career planning in an AI World, *Dr. Stan Schatt does an excellent job covering where these key technologies are, how they will evolve, and how you should adjust your short- and long-term career plans to take advantage of the coming waves best and avoid being buried by them. Being forewarned is being forearmed, and Stan's book will give you the information you need to ensure your future."*—**Rob Enderle, Principal Analyst, Enderle Group**

*"A well-researched and, at the same time, practical gem of a book on how to prepare for a future that is quickly evolving. What will matter most in the years ahead is agility and insights.* Still Room for Humans *is a must-read for those who are experiencing uncertainty and rapid changes, and eager to be smarter than other employees or investors."*—**Dan Ness, Principal Analyst, MetaFacts**

*"A truly captivating read on the impact of emerging technologies on your life, your career, and your world. For those at various career stages, this book provides critical insight on how your future will be impacted—and what to do about it!"*—**Barry Gilbert, Cofounder, Strategy Analytics**

*"In* Still Room for Humans, *Stan Schatt provides a wide-ranging, multidisciplinary, and thoughtful examination of the ways in which disruptive technologies such as artificial intelligence, robotics, and many others will transform our daily lives in the years to come. Schatt offers evidence-based observations, skillfully blended with business acumen and cultural insights, that provide historical context for our society's skepticism and anxiety surrounding*

*technological change, as well as relevant and timely recommendations on how a myriad of technologies can be effectively incorporated into a vibrant and socially responsible economy. The result is a balanced picture of the risks and rewards of new technology, together with a clear vision of career opportunities for the future and the best public policy to facilitate stable economic growth and social equity."*—**Clint Wheelock, Cofounder, Dash Network**

*"Understanding the future helps you plan better to meet the future. This book is a unique insight into the coming future that will help the enablers to accelerate our meeting this exciting future.*

*Mr. Schatt has a long history of consulting with big technology companies to help them understand the business future. In this book, he shares his unique insights into the future with all of us.*

*To many who see technology as a scary subject, this book demystifies the future in an easy-to-understand way. Mr. Schatt is a very good writer who is able to describe very technical subjects and make them easy to understand."*
—**Thomas Lobl, PhD, Entrepreneur in Residence, Alfred E. Mann Institute for Biomedical Engineering at the University of Southern California**

# Foreword

It's hard to ignore the clamor of experts warning that automation soon will eliminate millions of jobs and disrupt the lives of college-educated white-collar workers as well as high-school-educated blue-collar workers. Unfortunately, these same experts offer few answers to how workers could survive in such an environment where executives see dollar signs and greater orders of efficiency as good reasons for replacing workers with technology. It is likely many of these decision makers won't even consider the human cost of their actions, and their corporate lobbyists will make it difficult for the government to take punitive action to prevent massive layoffs in the private sector.

In the industrial revolution that took place during the period 1760 to around 1840, manufacturing moved from a cottage industry to large-scale factory production. Workers previously employed in agriculture became factory workers. A significant portion of American manufacturing moved overseas in the late 1980s as a result of globalization and the creation of a global supply chain. Many laid-off factory workers found jobs in the services industry that unfortunately for them paid far less.*

The presidential election in 2016 revealed that the social unrest caused by unemployment and underemployment as well as the view held by many voters that government does not really care about them could have enormous consequences. In fact, I devote an entire chapter to the ways government will have to change in the future to deal with massive disruptions in the country's labor market. It also will be necessary for people to push government officials toward labor-friendly policies as well as encourage educational institutions to adjust toward providing life-long educational training. Workers likely will need to retool themselves frequently to adapt to changing employment patterns.

---

* See M. Wooldridge. 2020. *A Brief History of Artificial Intelligence: What It Is, Where We Are, And Where We Are Going* (Flatiron Books), pp. 180–181.

My reason for writing this book is to help readers ensure that their careers and lives will prosper and not suffer because of automation. Although there are countless books available now on automation's impact on unemployment, they generally tend to fall into two camps. The techno-optimists point out that previous industrial revolutions have resulted in more new jobs being created than jobs lost after brief periods of adjustment, and they see no reason why this new period of disruption we are now entering should be any different. One example they often offer is that the creation of the Internet resulted in twice as many new jobs as it destroyed.[1]

Another example these optimists point to is that new technology has always resulted in the creation of new types of jobs that never could have been imagined in the past. Imagine explaining to someone in 1980 that in 2020, major corporations would pay their employees staggering salaries for analyzing social media coverage, or that people would make their money by living online as cultural influencers. Explaining the value of a tweet to someone who never used the Internet would be a challenge in itself. Another challenge would be to explain to someone in 1980 that today an entirely new type of broker is beginning to specialize in selling the rights to digital works of art or that people would pay brokers to invest in digital currency *mined* by computers.

The techno-pessimists, on the other hand, see major differences in the impact of today's disruptive technology compared to previous industrial revolutions. They point to the loss of enormous companies such as Sears and Montgomery Ward that provided work for tens of thousands of workers and the fact that scores of very small companies replaced them and employed only a fraction of the workers who lost their jobs. These newly hired employees generally found that these employers offered less generous health insurance, and did not offer pensions. Techno-pessimists also point to evidence that the current industrial revolution has already begun eliminating white-collar jobs, something that never happened before. In fact, some statistics suggest that people with undergraduate or graduate degrees might be more likely to fall victim to automation than those with high-school educations. While this idea might seem counterintuitive, I'll explain in later chapters why it is probably correct.

When some analysts describe the disruption new technologies will bring to the job market, their conventional advice for students is to major in science and technology. While that might be fine advice for a subset of the population who love science, those fields are not for everyone. There's a reason some colleges offer the equivalent of *Physics for Poets* to help humanities majors meet minimum science requirements to earn a degree. Some pundits who work for companies who sell their consulting advice to corporations predict a rosy future for businesses that will not hire permanent workers because they will have their pick from a talent pool where workers hustle from gig to gig and no longer expect any benefits from their contract employment. They describe a future where gig workers will fit into narrow niche jobs where it is inefficient to place machines and point to the opportunities for people to develop artistic creations for wealthy customers.

Other experts offer the comforting bromide that people shouldn't worry because workers and robots will coexist in blissful harmony as teams for the foreseeable future until eventually in the far distant future the machines prevail. That thought is not very comforting. Rather than accept the inevitable, it is still possible for people to control their own career trajectories by taking action today.

The first course of action is to understand what is driving automation. I examine the current status of artificial intelligence and robotics, the dual technologies that pose the greatest immediate risk to replace workers, and then offer some strategies for survival, including job opportunities these two technologies will offer. I also survey other emerging technologies that should offer new job opportunities for those people who are prepared to take advantage of them as well as other new technologies I describe later in this book such as augmented reality, 3D/4D printing, blockchain, green technologies, or CRISPR. In later chapters, I'll explain why technologies such as artificial intelligence, robotics, 3D printing, and virtual reality are so disruptive, offer timelines for when they will really impact the workplace, and suggest different ways readers can prepare themselves to find meaningful jobs in a changing workplace environment.

One of the keys to survival in a world where automation is increasing dramatically is lifelong education. I provide information for those in the beginning phases of their careers as well as those in mid-career. I coauthored a book titled *Paint Your Career Green* a few years ago. It showed readers how to take their existing skills, validate some knowledge of green technology, and then move into the green industry where job prospects continue to look very encouraging. My premise then as well as now is that there is no need for people already in white-collar jobs to go back to school to earn another degree. There are a number of ways today to validate enough knowledge about an emerging technology to become a valuable asset to a company embracing that technology even for nontechnical positions in areas such as accounting, marketing, or HR.

Finally, many experts point to a set of *human skills* that will enable some workers to become very valuable even for those companies that are planning automation. I describe those skills and then also show readers how to validate their abilities in those areas. This is a particularly important consideration for people already in the workforce.

I even have some advice for those people who work in positions where they don't feel they have much autonomy and room to broaden their set of tasks to prepare to survive automation. Even for those readers already in the workforce, it is imperative to develop career plans that take into account how to survive automation. I devote a chapter to this topic. Throughout the book, I point out the impact of technologies on specific industries as well as mention specific companies that offer products to automate tasks in those industries.

While I hope my readers will learn the skills necessary to survive automation, the problem of worker displacement is serious enough that I provide a chapter that describes some possible solutions the government could take, especially if voters put pressure on officials to develop worker-friendly programs.

So, rather than talk readers out of their career and industry choices that reflect their interests and passions, I want to prepare them so that they can prosper despite technological change. Let me provide an example. Let's say George really does want to teach elementary school even though he is aware that several emerging technologies likely will change a teacher's daily life when school districts embrace them. He might decide after reading this book that he wants to demonstrate enough knowledge of virtual, augmented, and mixed reality technologies so that he could become a very valuable part of the team that introduces the technology changes that inevitably will sweep across his school district. George would not have to train as an engineer in order to know enough about the technology to be a key part of a team that incorporates that technology into the classroom and ensures that it is consistent with the curriculum teachers want to come alive for their students. He might choose to train other teachers or develop curriculum that incorporates robot tutors.

Many people reading this book will at one time or another in the future wind up in a job that does not even exist today. I worked for two decades in a job and in an industry, neither of which existed when I was a college student. Few people in the future will work for the same company at the same job for 30 years. I've been fortunate in having been able to move from industry to industry by convincing employers that my skills from previous jobs in one field were applicable to new jobs in another field. So, I'm going to offer some advice on how to cultivate *soft* skills to go along with specific knowledge of various technologies. In fact, workers will need to become accustomed to the prospect of lifelong learning and constantly updating their skills and knowledge.

What should be encouraging is that any time a new technology begins impacting businesses, it takes a few years for colleges to formalize majors in these new areas of learning. While artificial intelligence and robots have both been around long enough for colleges to develop undergraduate and graduate majors in those fields, it is still too early for a company's HR department to require a degree in augmented reality or additive manufacturing (3D/4D printing) because it wouldn't have any applicants because colleges always lag a few years in developing formal coursework for new technologies. That means a person with enough initiative to learn about the technology has an excellent chance to get in at the ground level.

While some emerging technologies are so complex that graduate degrees are required for positions in engineering, keep in mind that the vast majority of positions within a company, particularly those in marketing, operations, sales, and finance, do not require engineering or science degrees. HR departments do hire people qualified in those nontechnical disciplines and likely will give preference to workers who understand the new technologies and are enthusiastic about working in a hybrid environment along with machines and sophisticated software. Let's say that Sue is graduating with a degree in accounting and wants to work for a company that takes climate change seriously. She made sure to take a few courses in environmental accounting. That background will give her a leg up on most candidates because she comes armed with the knowledge of how to calculate a company's cost of environmental compliance, how to calculate the use of alternate chemicals or product designs, and how to account for sale or trade of carbon credits.

I hope this book will provide a roadmap that will enable readers to future-proof their careers from the disruption new technologies are likely to bring to the labor market. In addition to descriptions of these new technologies, their state of readiness, and their likely impact on specific industries, I also have included examples of training opportunities as well as naming some of the current leading companies in these fields. For readers still in school, I hope this book will provide advice on some courses to consider adding before graduation. For those readers already in the workforce, I hope this book will provide advice for them in modifying their existing career paths to make them future-proof and ensure they are well equipped to handle the complex work world of the 21st century.

# CHAPTER 1

# This Time, Change Will Be Different

Let me begin by being completely honest. No one can accurately predict the future. During the late 1890s, a reporter writing in *The London Times* looked at the tens of thousands of horses in New York City and forecast that the city would eventually be buried in horse manure.[1] If the automobile hadn't come along as a disruptive technology that transformed the transportation industry, the reporter might have been right. No one could have forecasted how rapidly this technology changed everything. I assume someone who made buggy whips for a living never felt threatened by talk of *horseless carriages* until the buggy whip market suddenly collapsed. People in power are often the very worst prognosticators because they are comfortable with the *status quo* and often lack the imagination to conceive of a world picture different from their own. The famous scientist Lord Kelvin said in 1895 that, "heavier-than-air flying machines are impossible."*

In fact, the *Jetsons* television show that was popular during the 1960s, provided lots of examples where the inability of people to think outside the narrow range of form factors of what currently exists at the time makes it impossible for them to anticipate disruptive technology. The Jetsons' mode of transportation was a car much like cars of the early 1960s, only with wings attached. For large companies, the inability to anticipate disruptive technology can mean total ruin. Research in Motion, the company that dominated the corporate cellphone market with its Blackberries, is an excellent example. Steve Jobs introduced the iPhone,

---

* "Remarks by Deputy Administrator Gregory, Centennial of Flight Commemoration." December 17, 2003. NASA.gov. www.nasa.gov/audience/formedia/speeches/fg_kitty_hawk_12.17.03.html (accessed April 25, 2022).

a radically different way of communicating, and the Blackberry is now buried in the dustbin of history.

In fact, well-respected authorities throughout history have often warned against the dangers of disruptive technology. Pope Urban II during the Middle Ages warned that the invention of the crossbow could bring about the end of civilization and threatened to ex-communicate any Christian who used that doomsday weapon against other Christians. In 1589, William Lee proudly presented Queen Elizabeth with his idea for an automated knitting machine. He hoped for a patent, but was shocked when Elizabeth told him that his invention would result in too many of her subjects losing their jobs and might cause mass unemployment. Lee had to flee England or risk losing his head.[†] Nineteenth-century anti-technology mobs of people known as Luddites reacted to the threat to their jobs posed by automation by destroying automated textile looms. Today vandalism of electric cars and electric charging stations has been attributed in part to people who fear that technology will cause them to lose their fossil fuel-related jobs.

If so many people have been wrong in the past when it came to antic-ipating the impact of disruptive technology, why should anyone take seri-ously the warnings from experts that the next industrial revolution will be different, and that truly disruptive technologies will bring about enough automation to cause massive unemployment? The answer is that while in the past it has been a single technology that brought about changes in a particular industry, today, artificial intelligence and robotics have matured to the point that their impacts are likely to be felt on several different industries. At the same time, other emerging technologies soon will also make their impacts felt. California already has set a target date to phase out the sale of new gas-powered automobiles while builders are making enormous progress in technology that enables 3D printers to *print* actual buildings.

People generally assume it will be blue-collar manufacturing jobs lost when they read that technology might eliminate jobs. After all, robots

---

[†] Cited in C.B. Frey and M.A. Osborn. September 17, 2013. "The Future of Employment: How Susceptible Are Jobs to Computerisation?," *Oxford Martin Programme on Technology and Employment*, p. 6.

rather than people now paint cars on automobile assembly lines. Iron-ically, outsourcing and the creation of global supply chains beginning in the 1980s have already decimated the U.S. manufacturing sector to the point that it now only represents 10 percent of the country's work-force. So, rather than blue-collar workers taking the brunt of automation's impact this time around, it is likely to be white-collar workers in several other industries. Finance is an example. An increasing number of trades on Wall Street are now being performed electronically at the direction of artificial intelligence. A startling example of this trend is that the num-ber of traders working at Goldman Sachs' Equity Trading group dropped from 600 in 2014 to two in 2017.[2]

In the past when workers lost their manufacturing jobs, they moved to service industry jobs, but automation is now threatening those jobs as well. Driverless cars and trucks are progressing to where they eventually will be able to replace truck drivers and taxi drivers. China already has been experimenting with driverless taxis, while San Francisco now allows driverless taxis between 10 pm and dawn. Pizza companies are experi-menting with automated pizza delivery vehicles. Employees with college degrees used to dismiss any fear of automation replacing them because they held white-collar jobs in law, finance, insurance, health care, and so on. I'm going to give numerous examples in later chapters to show that jobs in those industries won't be safe much longer. The good news is that there are ways to survive automation, and I will explain how. Automation also will create new jobs for those workers who are prepared. That also is a major theme in this book.

New technology does not appear on the scene overnight and instantly kill jobs. It's a gradual process that begins slowly and then accelerates dramatically when conditions are right. Remember the story of the frog in a pot of water that is gradually heating up? Imagine now that same frog as a white-collar employee who imagines smooth sailing career-wise because he has a degree from Frog University and is happily employed in a well-paying job. In his mind, the path from junior executive to senior executive should be smooth. Pity that poor frog because he doesn't under-stand his skills are unremarkable and easy to automate. His inability to sense change makes his situation even worse. It doesn't matter if he's a highly compensated white-collar frog with a corner office bog. He sits happily in his spacious watery office and doesn't realize that new technology is gradually raising the water's temperature. By the time he finally becomes aware of his problem, it will be too late.

Change is all around us, but most of us are not aware of new technology trends because we tend to ignore gradual changes. Initially, only a few early adopters owned the first primitive smartphones, and the ones who did complained about numerous technical glitches. All of a sudden, though, almost everyone owned one. I headed a large research department before the Internet, and search engines became common. A teenager asked me how my department could possibly have done research before Google. Keep in mind that this search engine company wasn't even founded until 1998, so this teenager could not imagine how people managed without search engine technology less than 25 years ago. How many other technologies might change the world in far less than that time?

Gradual changes quickly add-up to major changes in daily and corporate life. In retrospect, of course, the changes over the past few decades have been profound. Think of a typical corporate office in the 1970s or 1980s and then compare it with one today. One way to do this is to watch a movie such as *All the President's Men* that was released in 1976. In that world, managers had secretaries. The sound of typewriters and landline rotary phones echoed through their offices while secretaries typed managers' memos. Clerks sorted voluminous stacks of mail (and not e-mail) before hand-delivering the letters to employees. People pulled into gas stations where attendants pumped their gas, checked their tires, and looked under the hood. People carried pagers to keep in touch with their offices and called in for messages from phone booths. Live operators helped facilitate their calls. Companies had their own internal travel departments that made arrangements and printed actual plane tickets. Personal computers and e-mail were still in their infancy.

While secretarial positions disappeared when managers began typing their own memos on their personal computers, technology created new jobs for PC managers and later for network managers and security professionals as well as for software developers and computer salespeople. Secretaries with computer skills became administrative assistants. While employees in the fax machine industry lost their jobs, new companies and industries emerged to offer e-fax services. Technology often develops rapidly during crises. Zoom was not a household word before COVID-19 changed everything. While most people no longer buy greeting cards to keep in touch, new jobs have emerged in the social media industry as corporate executives worry about their images on Twitter, Facebook, and Instagram.

The emerging technologies I discuss in this book will change the work landscape even more dramatically than past innovations. Roy Amara, a Stanford computer scientist, told colleagues during the 1960s that he believed that we overestimate the impact of technology in the short term and underestimate the effect in the long run. This phrase has become known as *Amara's Law*.

I often forecasted the success and failure of various technologies for the technology companies that hired me as a consultant during my two decades as an industry analyst. I had to be right far more often than I was wrong. What I learned early on was that Amara was correct. There is an inertia when it comes to a new technology taking over in part because all business conditions have to be right before companies abandon older proven technology and/or replace employees with machines or sophisticated software. There are always early adopters who embrace the latest and greatest technology regardless of the cost, but for mainstream buyers, the technology has to be mature enough to do the job better than the older technology it will replace, and its price has to be compelling enough to make adopting the new technology a *no-brainer*. Still, we are at an inflection point right now where several emerging technologies are reaching the state of maturity and price points to where initially they likely will eliminate more jobs than they create.

There's a reason you probably have not seen very many parking lot attendants, secretaries, or elevator operators and why you probably will see fewer paralegals, bank tellers, tax preparers, and insurance underwriters in the near future. If a job consists of repetitive tasks with little complex decision making, the chances are excellent that artificial intelligence will decimate the human workforce in that field. Companies will restructure more complex jobs so that they become hybrid combinations of human and robotic tasks. We still have mutual fund managers on Wall Street, but we also have AI managing a large percentage of trades because it can look at mounds of data and see patterns that elude human eyes. Doctors will still talk with patients in the future, but they will rely on sensors to analyze vital signs and encyclopedic databases to match symptoms with the latest medical research results. They also will be more prone to schedule videoconferences to meet with patients as telemedicine becomes far more common.

Before panicking, let me say a word about my experience with forecasting for several of the global leaders in technology research. For many years, I made my living forecasting what technology would be like five years or even 10 years in the future. Technology manufacturers paid for reports that included my revenue forecasts and then used those numbers a number of different ways in their planning processes. My numbers tended to be more conservative than those offered by many analyst firms. One product manager told me that he used very rosy forecasts by another analyst firm when it came to attracting capital from investors, but he used my numbers for his actual planning. What I learned over the years and mentioned a bit earlier in this chapter is that disruptive technology takes longer to take hold than most people think. Personal computers are an example of this phenomenon. It took several years longer than many people in the industry thought for PCs to become commonplace. Part of the reason was resistance to change, but another reason is that people need a specific reason such as an attractive application to move them forward and make them change the fundamental way they do things. The early spreadsheet programs VisiCalc and Lotus 1-2-3 helped jump-start sales.

## Forecasting How Quickly Automation Will Replace Jobs

If you've ever wondered how many occupations there are in the United States or which ones are likely to grow or decline, the Department of Labor's *Occupational Outlook Handbook* is online (www.bls.gov/ooh/home.htm). Besides listing educational requirements for various jobs, the website also lists the tasks performed in those jobs. So, back in 2013, a couple of Oxford University researchers went through the over 700 occupations listed at that time, task by task, and determined that 47 percent were in danger of being automated because of their repetitive nature.[3]

As you can imagine, the paper they released caused an uproar not only for the sheer number of occupations listed as endangered, but also by the timelines. Some techno-optimists criticized the study of over 70 pages and pointed to some flaws including its prediction that among the people it assumed would be replaced by robots were fashion models, manicurists, barbers, and school bus drivers.[‡]

While the forecast that automation will ultimately displace 47 percent of American workers was likely too high for reasons I'll explain shortly, several highly respected consulting firms have done their own arithmetic and made their own estimates. Bain and Company's analysts point to a major upheaval in the American workplace by the end of the 2020s with automation eliminating 20 to 25 percent of current jobs and hitting the middle-to-low-income workers the hardest, while those highly compensated and skilled workers (around 20 percent) would benefit the most.[§] McKinsey's analysts predict that nearly 70 million U.S. workers would have to find new occupations by 2030. This could happen due to advances in robotics, artificial intelligence, and machine learning. The firm believes that by 2030, the demand for office workers, including anyone involved in administrative tasks, should fall by 20 percent, while up to 30 percent of people in jobs that require *predictable physical work* in fields such as construction or the food industry would lose their jobs as well.[4]

America has always been a country where jobs have disappeared and new jobs appeared. The *Occupational Outlook Handbook* now lists over 800 U.S. occupations. A study revealed that roughly half of all jobs in the American economy have been replaced by new jobs every 90 years.[5] In fact, a look at the occupations added to the U.S. Census between 1940 and 2018 reveals such additions as Airplane Designer and Beautician (1950), Engineer Computer Application and Mental-Health Counselor

---

[‡] "Artificial Intelligence and Robotics: From a Labour and Tax perspective." May 2018. cms.law. https://cms.law/en/bgr/publication/artificial-intelligence-and-robotics-from-a-labour-and-tax-perspective (accessed April 25, 2022).

[§] "How Renewable Energy Jobs Can Uplift Fossil Fuel Communities and Remake Climate Politics." n.d. www.bain.com/insights/labor-2030-the-collision-of-demographics-automation-and-inequality/ (accessed April 25, 2022).

(1970), Artificial Intelligence Specialist and Chat Room Host/Monitor (2000), and Wind Turbine Technician and Sommelier (2010).[5]

Finally, industry analysts at Forrester, one of my former employers, divided workers into four categories based on their occupations and tasks and concluded that 29 percent of these people could be labeled *Automation Deficits*; that strikes me as a rather blasé way to dismiss over a quarter of this country's workers.[6] This study also categorized almost a third of workers as part of the *Talent Economy*. That's a rather nice way to describe people who have to try to survive in a gig economy, one that is great for employers that can take advantage of workers because they are contracted without benefits and not offered permanent employment.

One reason the forecasts are all over the place is because there is not a neat, accurate way to categorize present jobs. What if a robot could perform 70 percent of the tasks associated with a position? Would that be good enough for a company to replace the human with the robot? Other variables include how quickly companies would adopt automation. My personal experience as a consultant tells me that it always takes longer for technology to take hold than most technophiles would like to believe. Let me give you an example. I talked once with two engineers working at one of this country's leading silicon chipmakers. They discussed a faster graphics chip that would raise the price of computers. One engineer praised the chip and said he'd pay the extra money in a minute because it would speed-up the games he played at home. The other engineer agreed and said that the improvement in graphic quality was a *no-brainer*.

When I mentioned the new chip to people working in nonengineering positions at a major corporation, their reactions were far different. The added speed would not do anything for the basic productivity software they used, and the added cost would be enormous when multiplied by the hundreds of PCs they purchased for their company's many divisions. The engineers were technology lovers and classic early adopters who were willing to pay a premium for the latest and greatest technology. A *New York Times* reporter noted that off-the-record conversations with CEOs

---

[5] D. Autor, A. Salomon, and B. Seegmiller. n.d. "New Frontiers: The Origins and Content of New Work, 1940–2018," a lecture given at various times by the authors. https://economics.mit.edu/files/21810 (accessed April 26, 2022).

revealed to him that they had no compunction about eliminating jobs and improving their bottom lines through automation. What did slow them down, though, was the prospect of massive resistance by customers to reports that they were firing people and replacing them with software or robots. In other words, political concerns trumped business decisions.[7]

What makes automation this time so disruptive for college graduates is that AI has reached a level of maturity to where it now threatens middle-class white-collar jobs. Today's financial analysts might travel on automated elevators that no longer require elevator operators, and they no longer might hire personal secretaries, but their jobs have not changed much in decades, except that they now have computers and sophisticated software tools instead of calculators. In the near future many analysts are likely to be replaced by artificial intelligence. In fact, recent research reveals that financial services trails only high-tech and telecommunications companies when it comes to that industry's demand for artificial intelligence.[8]

In fact, if you think about it, the blue-collar workers who are still employed very likely have a better chance initially of fighting off automation than many white-collar workers. The reason has much to do with the limitations of today's robots. At the very worst, most of these workers will be needed to work collaboratively with robots for quite a while. I'll take a closer look at that subject in Chapter 3. The mantra most automation experts repeat today is that if a person's job consists of repetitive and predictable tasks and if these tasks can be described easily, then that job is probably in danger of being automated. Think of all the white-collar jobs where an employee asks several questions, gathers the information, and then comes to a conclusion as to what to offer the customer. A simple flowchart program directed by artificial intelligence software could lead customers to the same conclusions.

Take auto insurance as another example. Once potential customers provide information on their driving records, driving habits, and preferred amount of coverage, creating the price estimate is a very mechanical and repeatable process. Think of all the white-collar jobs in the health insurance industry. One job very much in danger of being automated is the individual who matches medical charges against health insurance coverage. Someone who shuffles papers all day and has limited decision making but instead has to rely on company policies and rules is very much in danger of becoming a victim of automation.

The cognitive dissonance out there on the speed of automation and the number of workers that will be displaced is amazing. The techno-optimists point to past industrial revolutions and, crossing their fingers, promise that jobs no one has even thought about will be created in time to help workers displaced by automation. The techno-pessimists, on the other hand, point to a future where all but the few who support the new technologies will be unemployed. The author of *The Robots Are Coming!* Illustrates my point. He devotes most of his chapters to examples of industries where robots will replace people including bankers, journalists, entertainers, and so on.[9] Techno-optimists, on the other hand, point to all the tasks only humans can do and see a world where humans and robots coexist. In *Present Future: Business, Science and the Deep Tech Revolution*, techno-optimist Guy Perelmuter concludes his book after chapters describing the wonders of most of the emerging technologies by telling his readers that, "The future is not only present. It is a present. Use it wisely."[10]

New technologies do produce new jobs, but the presently unanswered question is whether these technologies will produce jobs fast enough to make up for the jobs they automate. The past two decades seem to support the idea that it takes a while for a new technology to mature to the point that new jobs in large numbers develop. Take the PC industry as an example. It is only after the hardware and software matured that the computerized game industry really took off. It's one thing if the level of hardware and software sophistication permits the creation of a game like *Pong* that consisted of bouncing a ball back and forth. It's quite another thing when software developers can create games with realistic-looking people who can move naturally and even speak. Similarly, salespeople who used overhead transparencies for their presentations had to wait until computer processors and graphic chips were fast enough for Microsoft developers to create PowerPoint software. At one time, personal computer word processing software displays could not keep up with people who typed too quickly. The screen's display would lag far behind what was already typed.

So, depending on whether you choose to believe an optimist or pessimist, net jobs in the future might decline anywhere from 15 to 45 percent.

Based on my years' experience forecasting technology, I believe the truth falls in-between, particularly if you factor in people who might be under-employed to the extent that for all practical considerations, they might as well be unemployed. I also believe that the worst unemployment impact will be in the short term before new technologies are mature enough to generate new jobs and our educational system has adjusted enough to produce workers who are trained for these new jobs. So, that means the 2030s should be a lot more difficult for people than the 2040s, assuming world governments get a handle on climate change.

When executives were polled on their plans for automation, 75 percent of them responded that AI will be actively implemented in their companies within three years.[11] That sounds pretty ominous for white-collar workers, particularly if major portions of their jobs consist of repetitive tasks that follow easily programmable rules. Techno-pessimists see massive implementation over the next five years with immediate loss of jobs, while techno-optimists believe that there will be a period in which machines and people will work together on tasks, and the machines will only gradually take over completely. That leaves lots of time, they assure us, for workers to be retrained.

I believe the real future lies somewhere in between those two perspectives. Some job loss caused by disruptive technology is taking place already, and the pandemic clearly has accelerated that trend. While people have been working out of their homes, some corporate executives have quietly begun automating various tasks. McKinsey reported that 67 percent of executives polled have accelerated their adoption of artificial intelligence and automation to help them remain viable and profitable during pandemic restrictions.[**]

I am not optimistic that worker retraining will take place as quickly as some believe, and I do think that there will be a period of major labor disruption. Having said that, though, I believe new jobs in completely new fields gradually will sprout and grow. I list several possible new occupations likely to flourish whenever I discuss a specific technology. How

---

[**] "How Remote Work Has Accelerated Automation." February 26, 2021. *fisherstech*. www.fisherstech.com/how-remote-work-has-accelerated-automation/ (accessed April 25, 2022).

painful the transition will be in the future will depend on how many people prepare themselves and future-proof their careers now as well as how much pressure people put on their government to provide resources to make this industrial revolution the least painful and disruptive possible. So, let's look at two possible futures as a wake-up call as to what is at stake. I've written a number of science fiction novels over the years, so please indulge me as I put on my science fiction hat and paint two very different pictures of life in the future.

## Spending a Miserable Day in 2050

This scenario assumes that corporate executives prioritized the profits gained through greater efficiency from automation over any concerns over the destroyed lives of workers that they laid off. It also assumes that government did not take enough preventative action, and most workers did not make a concerted effort to prepare themselves to coexist with machines and make themselves too valuable to be laid off.

Unemployment is now over 40 percent in this version of the future, and that tells only part of the story because so many people either have stopped looking or are severely underemployed and are working gig jobs that don't provide benefits or steady paychecks. American social structure in this scenario is very much like what historians describe when they write about medieval England. The digital elite, those with highly technical skills as well as those in management positions, live in fortified enclaves with robot security guards. Think of this elite class as the future aristocracy. They rarely venture out of their enclaves because of food riots and their inability to avoid beggars. With virtually no middle class left, the lower classes resemble medieval serfs looking for crumbs to dribble down to them from the upper class.

Unfortunately, even though the digital elite has plenty of disposable income, they often turn to robot servants rather than hire people for domestic work. After all, they point out that robots are a lot less trouble to manage. The government makes extensive use of artificial intelligence and facial recognition to identify and arrest mob ringleaders who challenge the *status quo*. Faced with so many domestic problems and a shortage of revenue because so many workers now are unemployed, the government has abandoned the space program and the idea of colonizing other planets. American ingenuity has been stagnating because the government has little money to promote research and development. The reason is that new companies promoting new products have little chance of being successful because buying power now is so concentrated in a relatively small number of people.

Government in this scenario failed to adopt green technology because corporate lobbyists managed to torpedo most meaningful legislation, including eliminating the subsidies on fossil fuels. Parts of North America have suffered climate damage as well with large swatches of Miami, New Orleans, Houston, and New York underwater, and most countries have closed their borders to lock out climate migrants trying to escape areas devastated by climate change. Much of the Middle East and Africa are now uninhabitable because of extreme summer temperatures that exceed 130 degrees. A conservative Supreme Court declared carbon credits unconstitutional and nixed several attempts to subsidize green alternatives to fossil fuels.

In this scenario, the chasm between rich and poor has grown even wider than in the 2020s because Congress failed to enact laws that would have provided a safety net for displaced workers by taxing corporations. Attempts to tax companies that utilize robots also failed, and an attempt to form a labor union representing all human workers failed because a conservative court ruled it illegal.

Because the government provides only limited unemployment assistance, the unemployed spend most of their time in virtual reality worlds to escape their current plights. Actual travel is limited because of the cost as well as because of border shutdowns designed by governments to keep out climate change refugees. Companies that used to profit from middle-class tourism now have had to limit themselves to marketing to a much smaller customer market segment composed of elites.

Portions of America have increasing numbers of *Robots Keep Out* signs as well as mobs attempting to destroy robot factories. The U.S. economy is suffering because it has long been based on consumer consumption. While the digital elite do buy luxury items, that does not help manufacturers who produce mass market items, even though most of their factories are automated. One lesson apparently forgotten by those in power in

2050 is that Henry Ford became successful in part because he increased the daily pay of workers on his Model-T automobile assembly lines in the early 20th century. Those workers then used their disposable income to purchase Ford cars.

The negative impact of climate change on health means that by 2050, the average lifespan in the United States has fallen despite the increasing availability of telemedicine and the extensive use of wearable medical technology. The masses also suffer from nutritional deficiencies. All in all, it is not a very pleasant day in 2050.

## A Much More Pleasant Day in 2050

That's enough gloom and doom for now because there is still time to achieve a much more pleasant future. In this scenario of daily life in 2050, the government did act in the early 2020s to try to reverse climate change and succeeding at keeping the increase in average temperature to one degree centigrade, the absolute minimum climate change scientists felt would be needed to prevent catastrophic damage to the planet. Quick action during the 2020s resulted in the construction of sea walls as well as desalinization plants. There still is some flooding in the southeast portions of the country as well as New York, and the Pacific northwest and California do have major forest fires during drought filled summers, but life is bearable. Innovative methods of carbon recovery helped improve the quality of air.

While the summers are hotter, the Midwest did not turn into a dust bowl, and there are no food shortages. Food culturing and 3D printing of artificial meat, fish, and chicken have reduced the number of cattle and consequently the amount of methane discharged while offering nutritional meals at a fraction of the cost. Some young people express horror that their grandparents actually ate meat and drove fossil fuel burning automobiles. The largely plant-based diet most people now consume has improved health and increased Americans' average lifespan.

An aroused electorate put enough pressure on politicians to force them to overcome lobbying and enact meaningful laws that forced corporations to pay taxes to subsidize people laid off as well as taxes on robots when they used them to replace human workers. Labor unions representing human workers have become a real political force. After staggering layoffs in the 2030s, mature technologies such as AI, alternatives to fossil fuel, including nuclear fusion, quantum computing, additive manufacturing, and augmented reality, now have created millions of jobs in entirely new categories and even industries. Space colonization and space tourism are proceeding, and they are creating new jobs such as asteroid miner that never existed before. Cottage craft industries have sprung up to meet the needs of the digital elite for expensive crafts as well as for niche products for middle-class customers in areas that are not cost-effective for robots to produce.

A major government effort in the 2020s to build out electric charging stations coupled with the maturity of autonomous vehicles and very high-speed Internet and cellular service have changed the nature of the suburbs. A significant percentage of workers have moved several hours from cities to enjoy far cheaper housing. Most people now work remotely. Government programs to subsidize the unemployed with basic universal income in exchange for volunteer community work has resulted in tighter-knit neighborhoods with plenty of child care and support services available. Business and government partnerships and pro-worker legislation have minimized job losses and provided incentives for companies hiring human workers.

Having survived the unemployment period that always follows a major industrial revolution, most people now feel a sense of optimism about the future because so many new jobs and careers are springing up from now mature technologies. A radical rebuild of the country's educational system now means that vocational and academic training are tightly tied together along with internships sponsored by businesses. The schools offer lifelong learning for workers and supplement these offerings with robotic tutors and virtual reality instruction. It is very common now for people to retool their skills through lifelong learning.

The more pleasant vision of life in 2050 is possible, and there is still time to minimize the damage of automation both on its impact personally on individual careers and its greater impact on the nation's economy. I've structured this book such that readers can first think about their own careers and then turn their attention toward the issue of what the U.S. government and its citizens need to do to create the more pleasant vision of life in 2050. In writing this book, I make it a point not to recommend certain careers based on what or what might now happen to specific industries. As I mentioned at the beginning of this chapter, I probably would be extolling all the lucrative jobs available in the buggy industry, including the upholstering of the carriages, the manufacturing of buggy whips, the manufacturing of those large wooden wheels carriages required, and the increasing opportunities for blacksmiths if I had written this book in the late 1890s.

I want to point out what happened when the first horseless carriages appeared, think of them as the emerging technology of the early 20th century. At first, these new contraptions were a novelty that only the wealthy could afford. Blacksmiths still found work and factories still turned-out buggy whips. As the technology increasingly took hold, blacksmiths and buggy whip makers found themselves out of work and ill-prepared for jobs in the growing automobile industry. What happened after a brief adjustment period? Mechanically inclined workers turned to repairing cars and factory workers began working on car assembly lines. Salespeople began selling cars instead of buggies, and accessory manufacturers turned to providing products for cars instead of buggies. People who used to work in stables caring for the tens of thousands of horses necessary before automobiles now found jobs in service stations or in roadside restaurants catering to people out for a drive.

While it is critical to understand the scope of the problem automation poses to individual workers as well as to the country, it is also necessary to understand the potential as well as the limitations of the major technology that now drives automation, and that's artificial intelligence. That's the subject of the next chapter.

# CHAPTER 2

# Artificial Intelligence

Artificial intelligence (AI) is a term used to describe when computers and machines mimic human behavior and simulate human intelligence. Because, by definition, AI-driven machines appear to make decisions like humans, it's easy to see why some notables, including Stephen Hawking, Bill Gates, and Elon Musk, have extrapolated far into the future and warned that once AI surpasses human intelligence, it might decide humans are a problem and are no longer needed. As I'm not writing science fiction at this moment and virtually every AI expert predicts that it would be many decades if ever before artificial intelligence will even match humans and even longer before they think for themselves, let's focus on how AI will impact automation over the next 30 years or so.*

## Robot Process Automation

We probably should differentiate between AI and what is known as robot process automation (RPA). This type of automation describes software processes that never vary, so they don't require any real intelligence, although they sometimes are lumped in when discussing AI's impact on automation. Here's an example to illustrate what RPA is and isn't. Accenture applied RPA to a customer's invoice processing. RPA simply followed the same procedure over and over again without ever having to give it any thought. Unlike humans, the software never grew bored or turned its

---

* That doesn't mean the U.S. government isn't concerned about unforeseen impacts of AI. See National Science Technology Council Committee on Technology (NSTC). 2016. *Preparing For the Future*, pp. 32–33. obamawhitehouse.archives.gov. https://obamawhitehouse.archives.gov/sites/default/files/whitehouse_files/microsites/ostp/NSTC/preparing_for_the_future_of_ai.pdf (accessed April 26, 2022).

attention to other things while it daydreamed. The result was a 70 percent savings in time, a 30 percent improvement in productivity over human workers, and 100 percent accuracy.[1]

RPA is a definite threat to white-collar workers who perform the same tasks without any variation such as taking information on one type of form and then simply transcribing that data to a different form that requires the same content. It also is possible to combine RPA with AI. Tom Davenport, a professor at Babson College, offers the example of AI algorithms that perform character recognition of handwritten notes and then RPA that inputs the text onto a webpage.[†]

## Narrow Artificial Intelligence

Narrow AI is perhaps the easiest form of AI to understand and explain. It describes AI that is limited to a specific task or set of tasks. When IBM's Deep Blue beat Gary Kasparov, at that time the world's number one ranked chess player, it could only play chess. Perhaps that's why automation specialists looking for places where machines can readily replace people, try to identify jobs where workers have a limited set of tasks and very little discretion. Those types of jobs represent the lowest of low-hanging fruit when it comes to automation. One example is language translation.

With narrow AI, the computer and its AI software can leverage its primary advantages over humans—processing speed and memory (storage). Take the popular TV game of *Jeopardy* as an example. IBM built a unit known as Watson that whipped through its storage to find information, utilized its set of AI rules, and *buzzed* when it determined it had at least a 65 percent probability of being correct. Watson defeated reigning champions Ken Jennings and Brad Rutter. When Jennings lost, he was quoted as saying,

> Just as factory jobs were eliminated in the twentieth century by new assembly-line robots, Brad and I were the first knowledge-in-dustry workers put out of work by the new generation of "think-

---

[†] Quoted in W. Knight. March 14, 2020. "AI Is Coming for Your Most Mind-Numbing Office Tasks." wired.com. www.wired.com/story/ai-coming-most-mind-numbing-office-tasks/ (accessed April 25, 2022).

ing machines." Quiz show contestant' may be the first job made redundant by Watson, but I'm sure it won't be the last.[‡]

Similarly, Dutch chess grandmaster Jan Hein Donner told reporters how he would prepare for a match against Deep Blue after it beat Garry Kasparov. He said, "I would bring a hammer."[§]

It's not just champions of games like chess and Go who are learning that their jobs can be automated. Workers with complex jobs are not safe from AI because of advancements in what is known as *machine learning*. Many years ago, AI professionals thought they could program machines to anticipate any possible situation and then have them react according to a set of rules. There are several reasons why this approach didn't work. It's virtually impossible for programmers to anticipate every possible situation or to anticipate how situations might change in the future. I'll explain a bit later the technology leaps that made it possible for the AI industry to develop sophisticated types of machine learning.

## Supervised Learning

Supervised learning is one type of machine learning. Using this approach, AI pros provide a correct dataset and a test dataset along with a set of rules or parameters. They then *teach* the machine by having it answer and then correct it when it makes the wrong choice. That often means adjusting the parameters frequently until the machine's accuracy reaches acceptable levels.

## Unsupervised Learning and Machine Learning

What happens, though, when it is impossible to imagine all possible parameters? Unsupervised AI consists of providing a labeled dataset and letting the machine come up with its own criteria rather than establishing

---

[‡] See K. Jennings. February 16, 2011. "My Puny Human Brain." slate.com. https://slate.com/culture/2011/02/watson-jeopardy-computer-ken-jennings-describes-what-it-s-like-to-play-against-a-machine.html (accessed April 25, 2022).
[§] Quoted in E. Brynjolfsson and A. McAfee. 2014. *The Second Machine Age: Work, Progress and Prosperity in a Time of Brilliant Technologies* (Norton), p. 189.

parameters. Finally, the most challenging level of machine learning today is known today as deep learning. In this case, the machine is given enormous datasets and then allowed to come to its own conclusions. Often the machine will identify patterns that escape human eyes. One example where deep learning has proven very useful is identifying fraud in insurance claims.⁵ The deep learning approach tries to mimic the way humans think by creating what is known as a neural network.

In a neural network, a set of nodes (much like human neurons) filter and weight data and pass that information to other sets of nodes, each time refining the information and criteria gathered. Sometimes as many as 100 layers of nodes are required to refine information to the point that the system can come up with viable criteria.**

An example of deep learning and neural networks in action took place in 2016 when Google's DeepMind group created AlphaGo, an AI system that defeated Lee Sodol, the reigning world champion of the ancient game Go using reinforcement training. A year later, the same group created AlphaZero, an AI system that essentially played itself 4.9 million times and learned on its own without any human intervention. This time, it defeated its human competitor by a score of 100-0.[2]

A company tasked with building a neural network for the navy hired me several years ago as a consultant. The project's goal was to create a neural network that could look at sonar data and determine which signatures represented mines (danger—stay away) and which signatures represented rocks (some danger but not catastrophic). As I remember, the result was a neural network that was 99 percent accurate, far more correct than the best human experts but still not absolutely perfect.

Deep learning is a step toward AI professionals' ultimate goal, the creation of what is known as general intelligence. That term is used to describe an AI system that can learn a variety of different things when

---

⁵ "Re-educating Rita: Artificial Intelligence Will Have Implications For Policymakers in Education, Welfare, and Geopolitics." June 23, 2016. economist.com, www.economist.com/special-report/2016/06/23/re-educating-rita (accessed on April 25, 2022).

** "The Return of the Machinery Question." June 23, 2016. economist.com. www.economist.com/special-report/2016/06/23/the-return-of-the-machinery-question (accessed April 25, 2022).

placed in different situations very much like a human. One example of progress in this field is the fact that Google's Deep Mind was able to learn to play 29 classic Atari games at human performance levels without any input, except for the various games' on-screen pixels.[3]

## Why AI Technology Suddenly Is Accelerating

AI has gone through several boom or bust periods, primarily because overly optimistic AI pioneers overpromised and then underdelivered products. For the most part, they failed to deliver because they underestimated the complexity of the problems they were trying to solve, and the hardware and software tools available were not powerful enough to meet these challenges. We're now in an AI boom period for a number of reasons. One reason is the enormous increase in processing power now available to crunch AI algorithms. Gordon Moore at Intel noticed in 1965 that the number of transistors in an electron circuit (essentially its processing power) appeared to be doubling every year. His observation became known as *Moore's Law*, and the phenomenon continues to this day. While we've reached the point where it is impossible to stick more chips on a circuit board, parallel processors overcame that obstacle. By 2009, scientists were using graphical processing units (GPUs) in parallel as key components of their neural networks.[4]

As scientists began using reinforcement learning to *teach* AI systems, large datasets became more and more important; the arrival of what is known today as Big Data came just in time to supply that need. Equally important, the price of storage continued to decrease each year. The combination of increased processing power, cheap storage, and large datasets arranged in layers of nodes composing a neural network meant that a four-layer neural network that previously took weeks to complete its tasks could now finish them in less than a day.[††]

The result of these advances in AI technology meant that accuracy improved dramatically. One example is image recognition test that humans generally performed reasonably well with only a 5 percent error

---

[††] "From Not Working to Neural Networking." June 23, 2016. economist.com. www.economist.com/special-report/2016/06/23/from-not-working-to-neural-networking (accessed April 25, 2022).

rate. AI improved from a 26 percent error rate in 2011 to a 3.5 percent error rate in 2015.[5]

## AI's Hidden Job Cost

While most automation experts point to white-collar jobs completely lost to automation, and I've already discussed some of those grim statistics, there is a hidden job cost to automation. An MIT study revealed that while implementing AI software systems did not result in the laying off entire teams of people, it did slow down hiring in relevant departments. An example of this phenomenon that the study cited was an insurance company that automated a number of functions. That freed up time for its insurance agents. The MIT researchers concluded that for the immediate future, there were still enough people uncomfortable talking to automated systems that human insurance agents were necessary, although the company did not have to hire any new people for that role. The researchers saw this as a temporary situation until younger people age and become the main demographic buying insurance as they are far more comfortable taking advice from software.[6]

## Jobs Artificial Intelligence Are Creating

It is important to remember that while experts do expect the current digital revolution to cost more jobs than it creates at least initially, it's also bound to create new types of jobs. A study of job trends revealed that more than 60 percent of the jobs performed in 2018 did not exist in 1940.[‡‡] AI, as in the case of any new technology product, will require trainers, business development managers, product managers, marketers, and salespeople. In addition, though, there will be enormous numbers of new AI-related jobs in various industries. AI in automobiles, not just self-driving automobiles, is a potential growth area for jobs. Nauto

---

‡‡ See D. Autor, A. Salomons, and B. Seegmiller. July 2021. "New Frontiers: The Origins and Content of New Work, 1940-2018." blueprintlabs.mit.edu. https://blueprintlabs.mit.edu/research/new-frontiers-the-origins-and-content-of-new-work-1940-2018/?nowebp (accessed April 25, 2022).

(nauto.com) is an example of just one such company. It develops an AI software *driver* for a behavior-learning platform that improves safety for a company's car fleets.

In education, for example, there will be a need for AI learning coaches, courseware creators for teacherbots, and teacherbot maintenance and repair personnel. The arts will require AI-savvy people to enhance work by artists, musicians, and writers.[§§] This type of collaboration between human and AI is likely to take some unusual turns. As an example, IBM's Watson wrote a cookbook with the help of humans at the Institute of Culinary Education. Titled *Cooking with Chef Watson*, the book leveraged Watson's enormous processing power to search through tens of thousands of recipes and determine patterns for what ingredients often are paired. One example of the unusual combinations Watson offered is a recipe for an Austrian Chocolate Burrito. Humans helped with the project because, as staff from the Institute of Culinary Education pointed out, Watson lacked taste.[7] Of course, the AI field will also welcome those with skills to use AI to enhance accounting and cyber security as well as determine the best uses of this technology in various manufacturing, warehouse, and health care environments. Figure 2.1 lists some of the future jobs that AI will create.

Autonomous vehicles represent an area where ultimately there will be large numbers of jobs lost through automation as well as some jobs added. The technology right now requires all kinds of software and hardware engineers and designers, but ultimately, AI autonomous vehicles will displace truck, bus, and taxi as well as ambulance and Uber drivers. Many futurists believe that people will come to realize that they no longer need to buy cars as companies will spring into existence that will offer vehicle sharing. The implications of fewer people owning cars are enormous. Jobs will disappear for automobile dealers, salespeople, and auto mechanics. Drivers would require far fewer parking structures, and that change impacts not only attendants (already a dying breed) but also the people who design parking structures, the construction companies that build them, and the cleaning crews that clean them. Police in the near

---

[§§] "Artificial Intelligence Creates More Jobs." 2018. beyond.ai. www.beyond.ai/news/artificial-intelligence-creates-more-jobs/ (accessed April 25, 2022).

- AI developer
- AI user interface specialist
- AI intellectual property lawyer
- Machine learning specialist
- AI trainer
- AI business intelligence specialist
- Corporate AI Ethicist
- Driverless Car AI software specialist
- AI deployment specialist

**Figure 2.1 Some future AI jobs**

future will need fewer, if any, parking enforcement officers to give parking tickets. Insurance companies are likely to need fewer adjusters to handle the paperwork associated with automobile accidents.

## Crossing the Chasm

The Gartner Group noted that only 10 percent of organizations reported in 2015 that they were already using AI technology or they would be soon. By 2019, that number rose to 37 percent.[8] This dramatic growth in interest in AI reflects a phenomenon known as *crossing the chasm*. Geoffrey Moore's *Crossing the Chasm*,[9] one of the classics when it comes to technology marketing, described the technology adoption life cycle in clear terms and identified the five types of buyers and their respective share of the potential customer base as innovators (2.5 percent), early adopters (13.5 percent), early majority (34 percent), late majority (34 percent), and laggards (16 percent). The *chasm* Moore identified was the gap between technology adoption by innovators and early adopters and that of early majority adopters. He pointed out that many technology products fail to cross that chasm successfully. For one thing, innovators and early adopters are technology enthusiasts who are not price sensitive. Customers making up the early majority in the case of AI are likely to be pragmatists who are driven by business needs and a concern for the bottom line. David Kellnar looked at the AI market in 2017 and proclaimed that this technology finally had crossed the chasm and made its way to the early majority. He pointed to a McKinsey Global Institute study that 75 percent of executives stated that AI would be "actively implemented to some degree in their organizations within three years." Kellnar also quoted a Gartner

Group poll that revealed that while in January 2016, the term *artificial intelligence* wasn't even in the top 100 searches, it was seventh by 2017.[10]

The growing interest in AI encompasses most industries. A World Economic Forum survey polled its attendees on the technologies likely to be adopted by 2025 by share of companies in different industries and reported that AI was cited the most by people in digital communications and IT (95 percent), financial services (90 percent), health (89 percent), and transportation (88 percent), but even those attendees in agriculture, the lowest reported industry, registered a surprising (62 percent).[11]

## AI in Finance and Banking

Bain's research team identified financial services as one area where there is intensive action in using AI for automation. One reason is that so many jobs in this sector are labor intensive and expensive (think white-collar workers). Among the specific tasks Bain's report identified as ripe for automation were mortgage loan processing and investment analysis. It pointed to machine learning systems that now perform the work of thousands of analysts.[12]

## AI in Marketing

*Forbes* polled 1,093 executives and found that they identified marketing, along with customer service and sales as the top three functions where AI could reach its full potential. In the case of marketing, the executives polled indicated they expected to achieve tremendous efficiencies by targeting and optimizing the impact of hefty investments they already have made to media, content, products, and digital channels.[13]

## Chatbots and Customer Service

A chatbot is a software application used to conduct an online chat conversation via text or text-to-speech, in lieu of providing direct contact with a live human agent. Microsoft used neural networks to build a chatbot in China known as Xiaoice that conducted 30 billion conversations with 100 million humans.[14] People talked with that chatbot using an iPhone's

Siri interface. Another interesting thing about Xiaoice is that it assumed the role of meteorologist and reported the weather with a female voice for a Chinese television station. This chatbot did three 90-second weather forecasts during a two-hour program and reported on local, domestic, and international weather conditions.[¶¶]

Chatbots are playing an increasing role in customer relations. Acquire's communications platform offers a chatbot that can answer most customer questions and free up time for its human colleagues. It also compiles data and analytics so that companies can learn which questions give their bots the most problems.[15] The argument chatbot companies make is that their products allow human customer service employees to provide next-level help after the chatbots provide screening by answering the easiest and most often asked questions.

Chatbots utilizing AI can do far more than answer customer questions. They can improve customers' overall website experiences to the point that they transform customer encounters from mediocre to compelling interactions. In fact, 90 percent of organizations are now using AI as the way customers first interact with their companies online.

The problem, of course, from a worker perspective is that this role used to be handled by entry-level human employees who used that position as training to move up in the organization.

## AI in Law

Law firms used to hire researchers to pore through dusty law volumes to find case law support for their lawyers' cases. Now AI algorithms scan through millions of documents and summarize what they find. The fact that natural language processing has progressed as far as it has means that humans can communicate verbally with AI systems as they once did with their research assistants.[16]

A number of AI software companies have focused on products designed for the legal profession. Their targets include checking

¶¶ "What Happened When a Chinese TV Station Replaced Its Meteorologist with a Chatbot." January 12, 2016. washingtonpost.com. www.washingtonpost .com/news/innovations/wp/2016/01/12/a-chinese-tv-station-replaced-its-weather man-with-a-chatbot-and-people-liked-it/ (accessed April 25, 2022).

background information (due diligence), actually forecasting the probable success of litigation (prediction technology), creating templates for common documents (documentation automation), analyzing IP portfolios (intellectual property), and handling lawyers' billing (electronic billing). These AI companies include Leverton (analyze data and place it in real estate contracts), ThoughtRiver (contract reviews), and TrademarkNow (conduct patent searching).[17]

## AI in Journalism

It's ironic that while journalists have been reporting the threat AI-driven automation poses to so many industries, AI also threatens journalists' jobs. *Forbes* uses an AI content management system called *Bertie* to identify real-time topics as well as offering suggestions for improving headlines and adding appropriate images.[18] The *Associated Press* uses *Wordsmith* software from Automated Insights to generate articles on corporate earnings and sports events. It should be pointed out that corporations use *Wordsmith* to generate corporate earnings reports.

This software has proven particularly useful for newspapers when it comes to turning statistics from high-school games into brief articles because there are far too many high school games for staff journalists to cover. Another software package, *Quill* from Narrative Science, also automates data from high-school sports events.***

## AI in Administrative Roles

Remember the busy administrative assistant who might have to spend an entire morning trying to juggle a dozen different executives' schedules in order to find a time when all could attend a meeting. That's changed now that a company by the name of X.ai has created digital assistants with the choice of a male voice (Andrew) or a female voice (Amy). They understand natural language and can be used to set up or reschedule meetings as well as provide customized messages to individuals. Many people have

***  See M. Ford. 2015. *Rise of the Robots: Technology and the Threat of a Jobless Future* (Basic Books), p. 84.

received e-mail from Andrew or Amy and had no idea they were communicating with bots and not real people.[19]

## AI in Sales

*SalesForce* is a product that offers a comprehensive customer relations platform. What is intriguing is that *Einstein*, its AI assistant, analyzes data and predicts what leads are most likely to be turned into sales and provides quarterly sales forecasts. If that wasn't enough, it also suggests additional sales processes that can be automated. *Einstein* has been built leveraging advanced machine learning, deep learning, and predictive analytics.[20]

While *Einstein* is now an AI tool that works with human salespeople to help them improve their performance, it is bound to have a larger role in the future as over time as today's younger people, far more comfortable communicating with software, gradually become the majority of customers.[21]

At the very frontier of AI-enabled software support is the analysis of customers' emotional connection with a company. Cogito uses AI to ensure that salespeople's responses to customers are more empathetic. The software analyzes hundreds of cues, including the word choice as well as the tempo and mood of a conversation between a company representative and a customer. Imagine what a difficult task it would be for a human charged with monitoring hundreds of customer interactions and then making recommendations to the company's customer service employees for improving their performances.[22]

## AI in Retail

Retail is one industry that has been severely ravaged by the COVID-19 pandemic, but even before that, it was suffering from online competition. Now automation is beginning to make inroads. The Amazon Go store opened in Seattle with automatic checkout. Customers scan QR codes on their phone and walk out with products without human intervention. RFID tags on shelves keep track of product inventory. Meanwhile, AI tracks the customers.[23] Sometimes when humans and AI must work together as a team, problems can develop. Some human workers in warehouses are having trouble adjusting to taking orders from AI software. An Amazon warehouse worker complained to the *Financial Times* she felt like a robot in human form when it came to having to obey directions from the company's software that directed her to follow a specific route to an item she needed to pick up to fulfill an order.[24]

Speaking of Amazon, that company uses AI to predict what products are likely to interest its customers. So, every time a customer purchases something, that item becomes part of the data AI combs in order to make recommendations on similar or related products.

There's even more opportunity for AI-based automation in the area of retail distribution. A Bain study of a retail distribution center with around 120 full-time employees revealed that the jobs of around 70 percent of workers at this particular facility could be automated. Among the tasks likely to be automated were the sorting and labeling of inventory and the packaging of shipments.[25]

## AI in Health Care

AI adoption in the health care industry is proceeding quickly. An MIT study concluded that every position in that industry based on paperwork and staffed by humans eventually would become obsolete.[26] A radiologist friend of mine described how AI software is now able to detect tumors much more accurately than doctors. The Massachusetts General Hospital has partnered with NVIDIA to use AI-powered machines for disease detection, diagnosis, and treatment. The programs make use of more than 10 billion medical images in radiology and pathology for machine learning purposes.[27]

Bain analysts did a case study of a medical facility and analyzed the potential for automation and what that would mean in terms of loss of full-time jobs. A department with around 60 full-time employees could be reduced to around 45 employees. The major reduction, as expected, would be in a category labeled administrative staff and other labor. The tasks identified for automation included billing, recordkeeping, and managing schedules as well as most payment, information updating, and electronic communications with patients.[28]

# AI in Manufacturing

Manufacturing far surpassed all other industries when it came to cost savings from AI automation. In fact, 37 percent of manufacturing companies saw costs decrease by up to 10 percent following AI implementation.[29] Siemens' gas turbines contain hundreds of sensors that send information to an AI-operated system that adjusts the turbines' fuel values to keep emissions as low as possible. Yet another example is in the steel industry where AI reduces milling scaling by 15 percent that results in a savings that run into millions of dollars.[30]

Quality control is a key aspect of manufacturing, and now AI is invading that area. Nokia has installed a video application in a plant in Finland that uses machine learning to identify inconsistencies in production and notify that assembly operator. Similarly, BMW uses AI to evaluate images from its production line and identify deviations in quality standards in real time.[31] This is a job that presumably humans with quality control job titles once performed.

# AI in Software Development

One group of workers that one would assume is safe from automation would be software developers. After all, no one would expect AI systems to write their own software, or would they? Jen-Hsun Huang, the CEO of NVIDIA, points to deep learning techniques and concludes that in some cases today, we already have *data writing software*.[32] Of course, one limitation in this area is that there is growing resistance from government entities to the lack of transparency in some AI systems. When an AI system uses deep learning to detect patterns unrecognized by humans, just how apparent are its results? The reason that this matter is now in the forefront of recent government discussions is some spectacular errors in AI systems.

The failure of an AI system to identify a black male and instead label him a gorilla is particularly upsetting to government officials as well as the fact that facial image recognition systems often used by law enforcement seem to have problems identifying members of various minority groups accurately. In fact, one test revealed that the software was

34 percent less accurate in identifying darker-skinned females than lighter-skinned males.[33]

## AI in Self-Driving Vehicles

There's an arms race to build autonomous driving vehicles. Google's self-driving cars have now logged more than 1,500,000 miles (300,000 miles without an accident).[34] AI plays a crucial role in self-driving vehicles because so much of safe autonomous travel relies on AI interpreting enormous amounts of data and then making accurate decisions based on road conditions. Micron estimates that autonomous vehicles will require 300 million lines of code, far more code than any other software platform. AI in an autonomous vehicle system will be processing data from more than one terabyte of storage.[35] Among the input the AI system must juggle are signals from the global positioning system, the light detection and ranging sensors, video input from camera that can detect traffic lights, road signs, and other road conditions, and ultrasonic sonic sensors that measure the position of object close to the vehicle, including curbs and other vehicles with parking. Perhaps that's one reason why makers of autonomous vehicles often first familiarize them with a particular driving location so that the system can then focus on actual traffic conditions.[36]

The Society of Automotive Engineers have developed six automation levels when it comes to evaluating the level of self-driving a vehicle offers:

Level 0    No animation. The driver performs all tasks.

Level 1    Driver controls the car, but vehicle-assist features might be included.

Level 2    Partial automation with automated features like acceleration and steering, but driver remains engaged with the driving task at all times.

Level 3    Conditional automation. The driver is a necessity but not required to monitor the environment. The driver must be ready to take control of the vehicle at all times with notice.

Level 4    High automation. The vehicle is capable of performing all driving functions under certain conditions. The driver may have the option to control the vehicle.

Level 5    Full automation. The vehicle is capable of performing all driving functions under all conditions. The driver may have the option to control the vehicle.

*Source*: National Highway Traffic Safety Administration (NHTSA). n.d. *Automated Vehicles for Safety.*


Some manufacturers like Ford and General Motors have only permitted their autonomous software to operate on divided highways, but Tesla has not made those restrictions, although it has warned its drivers using its latest version of its autonomous software to sit in the driver's seat so that they can assume control if necessary.

Google's self-driving car does not require human intervention, but it is not yet being sold. Tesla, on the other hand, already has sold a lot of cars. It advises its drivers to be vigilant while some of automated safety features activate when safety is imperative. As an example, its AI software will prevent a driver from steering into a lane when another car is in its blind spot. It also will apply brakes if it looks like a collision could result if it didn't. Recently, though, when some Tesla drivers have placed their cars into self-driving mode, the cars have crashed into parked emergency vehicles. The National Highway Traffic Safety Administration (NHTSA) is investigating 11 crashes of this type since 2018 and has opened an inquiry into 765,000 Tesla automobiles produced from 2014 to 2021, including models Y, X, S, and 3.[37]

Some AI experts question whether Tesla's approach of placing its drivers in a position to take control if necessary is a wise one. The reason is that they believe drivers will become so accustomed to the autonomous mode that they will pay less and less attention to the actual driving, and they will not be able to react quickly enough if their cars' automated system fails to respond.[38] This situation apparently has been the case with the 11 Tesla automobiles that plowed into parked emergency vehicles because of some glitch in their cars' software.

## What Is Slowing AI Adoption?

There are still some obstacles to widespread AI adoption. Well-publicized crashes of AI-driven driverless cars have dampened enthusiasm. Other examples that caused some businesspeople to have second thoughts about AI include Google's AI-driven photo organizing service tagging black people as *gorillas* and a jaywalking detection system in China that incorrectly accused a woman whose face appeared on an ad on the side of a bus.[39] Other issues associated with AI include a poll that only 54 percent of people say they trust companies to use data collected from AI in a way that is beneficial to customers, while only 39 percent of people polled say companies are transparent enough in detailing how they are using AI.[40]

Psychological and legal issues along with technology glitches will determine how fast people embrace self-driving vehicles. Besides the well-publicized crashes of such cars just mentioned, there are concerns about legal issues as well. Take insurance, as an example. Who is responsible if a self-driving car crashes? Is it the vehicle's manufacturer, the maker of key software or hardware components? If the car ignores a traffic sign because the sign is covered with graffiti, is the graffiti artist the one responsible?

One chicken or egg problem concerns automated cars coexisting on the road with cars driven by human drivers. Many of the accidents involving automated cars while they were on their test drives occurred because of unexpected actions by human drivers such as making an illegal U-turn in the middle of the street or slamming on their gas instead of their brakes. So, will the public accept a hybrid arrangement until eventually all automobiles are self-driving, perhaps except for some hobbyists who might want to drive on special driving courses reserved for human drivers?

## Overall Timeline for Autonomous Driving Vehicles

Most experts believe that it will be a decade or more before self-driving cars become the norm, although they are likely to appear before that in specialized environments such as military installations, factories, mining installations, and ports. Such locations would not require the software to navigate through city streets.[41] In fact, many experts believe that it could be self-driving trucks rather than cars that first appear in large volumes on our highways. The reason for this is that long-haul trucks will be doing highway driving rather than city driving, a much easier task for the software to handle. Truck companies might even have drivers meet the self-driving trucks as they exit highways so that humans can drive the last mile.

Aurora is a company that has been developing autonomous automobiles. It has targeted 2023 or 2024 for the appearance of its self-driving cars and its ride-hail self-driving cars for a year or two later. In 2019, it shifted its focus to self-driving trucks because its executives determined that autonomous driving trucks are now in the lead.[42]

## Self-Driving Vehicles Create Employment Opportunities

Cruise is a San Francisco-based company that focuses on building self-driving cars and deploying them for ridesharing. Its website (getcruise.com) at the moment I'm writing this chapter lists close to 100 job openings. What is intriguing is that the company needs the usual array of people with experience in HR, IT, finance, marketing, and engineering, a number of the positions also require AI-related skills. As an example, the company advertises for an engineering manager focused on machine learning infrastructure and for a senior product manager focused on autonomous vehicle behavior. It is likely that a growing market for self-driving vehicles utilizing AI will spawn a number of new companies such as Cruise.

Argo.ai (www.argo.ai) is another self-driving company, one of many that have sprung up around Carnegie Mellon University, which, like MIT and Stanford, have acted as incubators for new AI and robotics companies. On the day I was writing this chapter, I saw around 70 job openings, many of which required knowledge of traditional business disciplines but also required knowledge of AI. The point is that emerging technologies will create a number of startups that will need to hire workers. Whether these new jobs will be enough to make up for the jobs white-collar workers lost to automation in more traditional companies such as insurance and financial firms is an open question.

Aptiv (aptiv.com) is another company focused on electric self-driving cars. It is a spin-off of the bankruptcy of Delphi after it no longer was a part of General Motors. Its mission is "to find solutions to customers' most difficult challenges by enabling the transition to software-defined vehicles supported by electrified and intelligently connected architectures that will combine to power the future of mobility." Among its several businesses is one that focuses on autonomous vehicles. The day I wrote this chapter, the company listed over 700 job openings.

Companies not normally thought of as AI companies are jumping into the self-driving car business as well, mostly through acquisition. Spun out of Stanford's AI lab, Drive.ai was a company that specialized in AI used for self-driving vehicles. Apple purchased it in 2019, and it now is part of Apple's Project Titan. Rumors persist that Apple is planning to release a self-driving car by 2027 and is working with Hyundai. In 2017, Apple's CEO Tim Cook said, "We're focusing on autonomous systems. It's a core technology that we view as very important. We sort of see it as the mother of all AI projects. It's probably one of the most difficult AI projects actually to work on."[43]

McKinsey analysts believe that 95 percent of automobiles will be connected to the Internet by 2030.[44] That connection means that automotive manufactures will have a treasure trove of data about their customers. As far as job opportunities go, there is already talk about using that data to pinpoint specific drivers based on their data and then project targeted advertisements to billboards these drivers will pass on the road.[45] Imagine the new job opportunities for marketing and database personnel.

## Self-Driving Vehicles and the Trend Toward Electric Vehicles

It is important to keep in mind that the movement toward autonomous self-driving cars is preceding hand-in-glove with the movement toward electric vehicles replacing those cars and trucks that require fossil fuel. It is true that ultimately self-driving cars and trucks will have an enormous impact on employment because the jobs of so many workers, whether they drive taxis, buses, cars, or trucks, will be eliminated. The impact of electric vehicles will be even more profound. An MIT study group examined the issue and pointed to the impact on the entire ecosystem now associated with gasoline-fueled cars. That would include making and selling parts as electric vehicles have far fewer parts.[46] It is also true, however, that the explosive growth of electric cars will create new jobs associated with the batteries that power these vehicles. The expansion of companies making the various sensors that AI requires on self-driving cars will also add jobs.

While I've focused this chapter on AI software and its impact on automation, job loss, as well as job creation, AI is often combined with hardware, particularly in the form of robots. That's the topic of the next chapter. First, though, let's look more closely at the future career opportunities associated with AI as well as the preparation necessary.

## Artificial Intelligence Careers

Career paths are wide open right now for AI. College students interested in careers on the technical side can take a number of paths, including natural language processing, machine learning, and computer vision. AI careers can include work with robots as well as with large datasets used to train AI. It also can include work on the type of interface and interaction between human and machine. There a number of AI career paths depending on a person's interest. Data analytics is an area where people analyze patterns in data sets. Think of Amazon's recommendations that are based on its customers' buying histories and preferences. Data miners comb enormous datasets looking for patterns that can predict future behavior. AI software engineers build AI programs, while machine learning engineers grapple with how to help AI systems learn even more effectively. Knowledge of Python and C++ are important for AI software engineers.

## For College Students or Those Preparing for College

Students interested in a technical track often major in computer science, mathematics, or a math-related major such as economics. Courses in areas such as linguistics, neuroscience, or psychology can be very useful. Many colleges are starting to offer AI minors that serve as ideal credentialing for students who want to be knowledgeable enough to be users of AI in their chosen fields. For people interested in more than entry-level positions in a technical career in AI, a master's degree is very desirable, while a PhD is necessary for those interested in AI research.

## Major Centers of AI Instruction

In 2018, Carnegie Mellon became the first university to offer an undergraduate degree in AI, and Cornell, Georgia, and Columbia now offer this degree as well. While very few universities offer undergraduate degrees specifically in AI, a number do offer computer science degrees with an emphasis on AI. These schools include Stanford, Harvard, and MIT. The list of schools offering advanced degrees in AI is much longer.

## For People Already Employed
## Who Want an AI Career

For software engineers already employed, the transition to an AI career is not difficult. There are a number of online certificates and even some *bootcamps* that specialize in providing the necessary AI content to complement a programmer's technical knowledge of coding. Stanford University offers one of the most widely respected online certificate programs in machine learning that includes 61 hours of instruction through Coursera (Coursera.org). Eureka! (Eurekatech.org) offers a certification program in Python and machine learning that features classes online on weekends. One way to demonstrate AI programming ability after receiving such a certification is to post code on GitHub.com.

Because AI is impacting so many different industries, people already in the workforce who are not necessarily interested in learning programming can transfer their skills to an AI-related job by earning a certificate. Several different types of AI are available depending on what areas are of interest. At the time I wrote this book, Coursera (coursera.org) offered 1,352 different courses in AI, including many that focused on AI applications for different industries. edX (edx.org) and Udemy also offered a number of courses. In fact, Udemy offered 2,907 different AI online courses.

For managers, there also are short-term online or weekend classes that can offer the chance to become leaders when their companies adopt

AI technology. Many universities, including MIT, UC Berkeley, and the University of Texas, offer such programs where the emphasis is on business applications of AI and implementing AI. MIT's Sloan School of Management's Executive Education division, as an example, offers a short online course in AI in health care, while Northwestern University's Kellogg School of Executive Education offers a short-term program in AI applications for growth.

Google offers a number of courses in AI and machine learning (https://ai.google/education/). While the price of online AI certificates can vary enormously, one very reasonable way to gain AI knowledge for working professionals is their local community college where many certificate programs are offered in the evenings and on weekends. Maricopa County Community College in the Phoenix, Arizona area, offers a certificate of completion in AI and machine learning. It even teamed with Intel to offer the country's first associate degree program in this field.

Because AI is expanding so quickly into so many industries, there will be ample opportunity for people already in the workforce in areas such as supply chain logistics, retail management, IT, transportation, health care, education, and cybersecurity to package their industry knowledge and experience with an online AI certificate program to become indispensable to their companies. Keep in mind that people already employed in a field have the hands-on industry knowledge that graduates of AI degree programs lack. Much of what Michele Lobl and I wrote in *Paint Your Green* focused how to transfer current job skills in order to move to a green career also applies to moving to a career in AI. Remember that in addition to becoming instrumental in your company's adoption of AI technology, companies that sell AI products will need people in marketing, public relations, sales, training, and other areas that already have those skills and also have picked up enough AI knowledge from certificate programs and courseware to be invaluable.

# CHAPTER 3

# Robotics

Robots are programmable machines. Some surgery robots, as an example, perform the specific tasks they have been programmed to perform and do not learn on the job. When it comes to automation, it is important to realize that these machines can take a number of different forms and not just a human shape. In fact, it is humbling for some workers on assembly lines when they realize they have been replaced by what amounts to an automated arm that is ideal for performing repetitive tasks. Similarly, while some robots have artificial intelligence and even a subset of those are capable of deep learning, many do not.

## Robots Without Intelligence

Robots without intelligence are very common, particularly in industrial settings as so many tasks are repetitive and require no judgment on the part of the robots. Later in this chapter, we'll look at robots that work cooperatively with humans as well as those that are intelligent enough to work without human intervention.

Let's say that a worker by the name of Burns worked in a position known as a *toaster*. His job was to place bread in a heating device, closely monitor the bread's darkness, and then take it away from the heat before it burns. He's furious when he learns he's been replaced by a mechanical toaster and blames automation, but the point to be made is that the toaster is not an intelligent device. In fact, a large proportion of robots are not intelligent, particularly those on factory floors. A mechanical arm simply repeats what it is programmed to do. A robotic vacuum cleaner also does what it has been programmed to do. It doesn't come to an object it cannot recognize and ponder what the object is. It simply vacuums. People who lose their jobs to robots that lack intelligence probably spent a good portion of their workdays bored and daydreaming. Rather than bemoan the loss of such jobs, people need to focus on areas where human intelligence and agility surpass that of robots. That is the subject of Chapter 13.

## Cobots

For the foreseeable future, many people will find themselves working with robots rather than being replaced by them. Cobots are robots that are designed to work with people. What does that mean? It means in some ways, they have been modified so that they don't accidentally hurt human workers. They move slower, grip softer, and generally carry lighter loads so that they don't represent a threat to workers' safety.[1] Generally, humans can move the cobot's arms to demonstrate the action required and then the machine automatically adjusts the amount of force needed to perform specific tasks.* The downside of working with cobots is that they're not going to carry on a conversation about what they did during the weekend nor are they going to agree to meet after work and nurture a friendship. Built Robotics has partnered with a 400,000-member construction union to offer a training program to teach workers how to oversee and manage robotic equipment as well as work alongside autonomously operating vehicles.[2]

Robot companies can enhance their cobots by giving them some artificial intelligence. Veo Robotics, as an example, adds 3D sensing to its cobots so that they are aware if they are near humans. These cobots do the heavy lifting in an industrial environment and leave the tasks requiring more dexterity to human workers.[3] Robotiq produces cobots that have mechanical components that produce passive compliance so that if an external force acts on one of its joints, it will move in the opposite direction to avoid injury to a human. Similarly, some cobots only lift objects weighing one kilogram or less so that even if they dropped the load on a person, it would not hurt them.† Robust AI, a company founded by Rodney Brooks (founder of several other robot companies), now sells a

---

* All is not rosy for cobot manufacturers though. Rethink Robotics was one of the major players in this industry but closed its doors despite having raised $150 million from investors.

† *Robotiq, Collaborative Robot Buyer's Guide*, Version 8.1. May 2020. https://blog.robotiq.com/collaborative-robot-ebook (accessed May 1, 2022).

robot named Carter that is designed to read human body language so that it can figure out how to collaborate with human workers. Perhaps this is the next stage in cobots because Brooks believes that the ability for robots and humans to work together will create more jobs for humans.[4]

I should note, however, that danger still exists where robots, no matter how *human-friendly*, coexist with people. Recently, a robot playing chess with a seven-year-old child grabbed the child's finger rather than a chess piece and broke it.[5] The problem with such stories is that although they are very rare, they get a lot of publicity and could cause push-back on efforts to win acceptance of cobots.

## Factors Driving Sales of Robots

A number of factors are driving the growth of the robotics industry. More powerful processing power is a significant driver, as measured by computing power per watt of electric power. Also, advances in AI have given robots computer vision while natural language processing has increased their ability to learn.[6] Microsoft's Kinect, as an example, now offers an inexpensive way of giving robots three-dimensional machine vision. Also, companies such as CloudMinds are increasing the ability of electronic *brains* of robots by linking them to the cloud so that the robots' brains do not have to hold all necessary information.[7]

Other factors driving robot sales are the rising cost of human labor coupled with the decreasing cost of robots. A Bain study concluded that while the estimated payback period in China for replacing workers with robots had dropped to 1.5 years in 2016, the payback should fall to less than one year by 2030. FoxConn has replaced 60,000 of its factory workers with robots.[8]

## The Growth of the Robotics Industry

While the growth of the robotics industry is significant, it is far from uniform. Four manufacturing industries account for 70 percent of all robots in use in the United States. The leaders include the auto industry (38 percent), electronics (15 percent), chemicals (10 percent), and metals (7 percent). It is ironic that the use of robots in manufacturing lowers the cost of goods so that other industries benefit. The overall impact is that one robot replaces 3.3 jobs.[‡]

ABI Research estimates that more than four million commercial robots will be installed in more than 50,000 warehouses by 2025.[9] The new World Robotics 2020 Industrial Robots report showed a record of 2.7 million industrial robots operating in factories around the world—an increase of 12 percent.[§]

## Robots' Impact on Employment

University of Chicago researchers found that adding one machine per 1,000 workers resulted in a decrease in the employment rate of 0.18 percent. While that sounds miniscule, it corresponds to about a half of million layoffs in the United States.[10] Another study found that a 20 percent increase in robots in a given industry leads to a 1.6 percent decline in employment there.[11] It should be noted that the robotics industry would also generate new kinds of jobs as well. Figure 3.1 lists some of the future robot-related jobs on the horizon.

## Robots With Artificial Intelligence

We're conditioned from science fiction books and movies to imagine a humanoid-looking robot that stands on its two feet and has a human-like face. With some robots, that is the case. One truism is that the porn

- Robotics mechanic
- Robotics salesperson
- Robotics law specialist
- Robotics ethicist
- Robotics tutor specialist
- Medical robot designer
- Robotics engineer
- Robotics eldercare specialist
- Robotics deployment specialist
- Robotics business developer
- Robotics plant manager

*Figure 3.1 Some future robotics jobs*

---

[‡] Quoted in P. Dizikes. May 4, 2020. "How Many Jobs Do Robots Really Replace?" techxplore.com. https://techxplore.com/news/2020-05-jobs-robots.html (accessed May 5, 2022).

[§] International Federation of Robotics. September 24, 2020. ifr.org, Frankfurt. https://ifr.org/ifr-press-releases/news/record-2.7-million-robots-work-in-factories-around-the-globe (accessed May 5, 2022).

industry, criminals, and those skirting the law often are the earliest of early adopters of new technology. After all, porn websites dominated the bandwidth of the early Internet. One unusual example where sex can be linked to human-appearing robots is the creation of sexbots, female and male robots with artificial intelligence.

### Robot Sex Workers

While it would seem that the most secure human workers when it comes to natural protection from automation would be sex workers, it is simply not the case. Some houses of prostitution (legal in Amsterdam) have replaced their female workers with sexbots. Doll no Mori, a Japanese company, started a call girl service in 2004 that features dolls. It charges around $110 for a 70-minute session with the dolls with most customers requesting a two-hour session. The cost for a call girl doll is about the same as for a real girl escort. The company started with four dolls and made back its original investment on one month as it did not have to pay wages.[12] The Japanese call girl doll operation is not unique. Lumindolls, a sex doll brothel in Barcelona, advertises realistic dolls that have moveable joints and a texture that feels like real skin for the price of around 100 euros per hour.[‡]

The most challenging design issues for sexbot manufacturers have to do with the robots' bodies. Making them walk in a human-like fashion is very difficult as is the weight of these creations. For those reasons as well as many others, sexbot makers have chosen to start with perfecting the head. Abyss Creations (realdoll.com) has created the Harmony AI as a $10,000 platform. Harmony initially will work in conjunction with the sex dolls the company has sold for many years. In the near future, the company will add touch sensors, heating, self-lubrication, and vibration.

## Robots Delivering Products and People

The Chinese company AUTOX has been working on self-driving grocery delivery and already offers self-driving taxis that use AI software along

---

[‡] Cited in N. Sharkey, A. van Wynsberghe, S. Robbins, and E. Hancock. July 5, 2017. "Our Sexual Future With Robots," *The Foundation for Responsible Robotics.* https://responsiblerobotics.org/2017/07/05/frr-report-our-sexual-future-with-robots/ (accessed May 22, 2022).

with sensors and cameras.[13] In an earlier chapter, I pointed out that a number of workers who lost their manufacturing jobs migrated to the services industry and became cab drivers. Today, many people have joined the gig economy and drive for delivery services such as Door Dash. What happens when robots can handle these tasks? Already Agility Robotics is selling a robot named *Digit* for vehicle-to-door delivery of packages weighing 40 pounds or less.[14]

## Industrial Robots

While more robots are found in the manufacturing industry than anywhere else, 40 percent of those robots are found in the automotive sector.[15] While this enormous percentage of the total number of robots deployed is impressive, it masks a basic weakness of robots designed for industrial purposes. Much like a wide receiver that drops every other pass but looks very impressive if you just look at his physical characteristics such as speed and size, robots' hands are currently the weakness that is holding them back. While people can use their hands to grip countless items and can adjust to apply just the right amount of pressure, robots still require multiple sets of grippers to handle different situations. Until robot manufacturers can come up with an all-purpose gripper, robot growth in the industrial sector will be limited. Today, human workers need to handle tasks requiring dexterity. Unfortunately, time is on the side of the robots as manufacturers continue to make progress.[16]

## Robots in Warehouses

One major use of robots today is in warehouses. Amazon purchased the robot company Kiva in 2012. As of 2019, the company had more than 100,000 robots working in its distribution centers.[17] Robots in warehouse environments generally locate, lift, and carry items to areas where humans complete the picking process. Covariant is an AI-based robotics company that has developed robots that are able to *learn* how much pressure its grippers should apply to specific objects it lifts. The result is that industries such as fashion, beauty pharmaceuticals, and groceries are starting to add robots to their warehouses where they work along with human workers.

Warehouses still require human workers for delicate tasks such as auto-bagging where flimsy materials often are used. Still, with industry analysts predicting the need for tens of thousands of robots in warehouses the next several years, even the most optimistic forecaster predicts that it will be several years before warehouses can rely solely on robots. One solution for the present often found is to design warehouses with certain areas set aside for robots, while other areas are designed for humans and their needs.[18] An IBM Institute for Business study concludes that when robots finally become able to displace warehouse workers, those humans should transition to other warehouse jobs that require *higher skills* such as thinking and complex movement.[**]

## Robots in the Retail Industry

It's hard to believe that just a few years ago before Amazon and the Internet, the retail industry served as a major source of employment. Now malls are dying as their *anchor* tenants are going bankrupt. A new type of retail store is emerging, one without human workers. This type of outlets can take different forms. One form is a number of self-service vending machines and kiosks. Who would imagine a few years ago that people could or would feel comfortable enough to make a major purchase such as an iPad from a vending machine? People now can visit a Robofusion kiosk and order ice cream using a touchscreen to indicate their preferences for toppings, and the robotic dispensers produce the product without human intervention.[19] While Amazon has opened a retail store in Seattle that does not need human workers, at least for the immediate future, robots will coexist with employees in retail establishments.

One practical function for robots in retail stores is to offer directions to shoppers looking for specific items. Lowe's LoweBot is an example of this type of robot as is Pepper, a robot at HSBC Bank who can explain various banking services and, when necessary, direct customers to the appropriate person to help them.[20] One common function for robots in retail stores is to scan shelves. Some robots can identify items that are

---

[**] Cited in M. Thomas. 2022. "The Future of Robots and Robotics."

shelved incorrectly as well as alert human workers of items that need to be reordered ahead of schedule because of demand.

We are not likely to see supermarkets without human workers to any great extent for the foreseeable future, but Amazon Go is an exception. It is a cashier-less supermarket with humans only serving as greeters and stock associates, while other functions such as checkout and security are handled by artificial intelligence.[21]

Retail grocery stores are one area with coexistence is certainly the case. Ahold Delhaize is deploying 500 robots from Badger Technologies. These six-foot robots roam aisles looking for spills and alerting workers of hazards.[22] Even though most grocery stores now have self-checkout aisles, many people hate these because there is no discount for shoppers to do the scanning work themselves. A researcher who has studied the phenomenon calls such automation *so-so automation*.[23] It is barely good enough to do the job as now a harassed grocery clerk usually is responsible for keeping an eye on self-checkout aisles to help frustrated shoppers. The problem is that *so-so* automation has the impact of slowing the hiring of human workers.

Even when robots and humans currently coexist in a retail environment, the robots can reduce the workers' quality of life. Walmart has installed robots in more than 1,500 of its stores. Workers have named a robotic floor scrubber *Freddy* after a janitor that the device replaced. Workers claim the machines send alerts to them via handheld devices when the robots detect a problem. The human workers then hurry to address the issues the robots raise. They complain that they find it demeaning to have to respond to these machines' commands.[24] Similarly, the Marty Mobile Robot deployed at Stop & Shop, Giant Eagle, Schnucks, and other grocery stores transmits information to human workers as to which shelves need to be restocked and which products are in the wrong location.[25] I'm sure that a human worker is bound to ask if the robot is so intelligent that it can figure out that something is in the wrong place, why can't it pick up the object and move it to the proper location? I conducted a focus group on a very large, complex, and expensive printer. When the printer ran out of paper, even in the middle of the night, it would call an IT manager at home and, in its mechanical voice, ask that person to come back to work to load it with paper. The reaction of IT managers was as expected: "If it's smart enough to call me, it should be smart enough to load itself with paper."

## Robots in Restaurants

Automation is making some strides in restaurants, due perhaps to the shortage of workers as a result of the pandemic. McDonalds and other chain restaurants have introduced terminals for customers to place their own orders. Peanut is a robotic waiter who can assist human workers in bringing food to a customer's table. It still is quite limited, though, as it cannot take orders or physically hand plates to customers. While Peanut can sing Happy Birthday to customers, a human has to press its button to initiate the song.[26]

Kura Sushi, a chain of sushi restaurants, has taken an even more radical approach. Robots make the sushi and rice balls, and conveyor belts replace human workers.[27] Moley Robotics produces Moley, a headless robotic chef with multiple robotic arms who is able to prepare 100 different recipes.[28] Because the pandemic has put a halt to do-it-yourself salad bars, there is likely to be greater demand for robots like Chowbotics' Sally unit. At Holy Cross' Hogan Campus Center, the robot prepares customized salads for students after they have selected their preferences.[29] Commercial kitchens also are adding robotic chefs. The Los Angeles Dodgers utilize Flippy, a robot from Miso Robotics, to cook and serve chicken tenders at Dodger Stadium.[30]

Remember when working in a fast-food place flipping hamburgers used to be a typical first job for a teenager? Momentum Machines, a fast-food restaurant in San Francisco, is deploying a hamburger-flipping robot to handle that task. All the hamburgers are uniform and cooked to the same degree. The robot never daydreams or is distracted when a pretty girl visits the restaurant.[31]

## Robots in Health Care

Robots are beginning to assume a number of different roles in hospitals. Diligent Robotics' Moxi serves as a helper for nurses and health care workers. The company found that nurses spend 30 percent of their time gathering supplies and information, so this robot provides that functionality as well, which permits nurses to spend more time with patients. Nurses can page Moxi from their phones when they need supplies. Intuitive Surgical's DaVinci robots have performed over 8.5 million operations.[32] Owing in part to their ability to provide 3D visualization during surgery, these robots have been used to treat prostate cancer and now help perform lung biopsies.[33] Xenex is a robot that disinfects hospital facilities using ultraviolent light, while Accuray's robots employ a variety of arms to administer radiotherapy to various parts of the body, including the pancreas, lungs, and brain.[34]

## Robots Helping the Elderly

Americans can view the current eldercare crisis in Japan and get a preview of what they likely will face in the near future. The Japanese population is aging at an incredible rate with approximately a quarter of its population over the age of 65. A declining birth population means that there will not be enough younger people to care for seniors. Today, in the United States, 10,000 boomers are turning 65 each day. Over the next 30 years, the population of older adults will almost double from 48 million to 88 million, with the largest percentage increase among those 85 years and older. Over the next decade, there will be a need for hundreds of thousands of additional home care workers.[35]

The problem is that home care is a very low-paying profession that is not likely to attract new workers. So, as the elderly become a larger share of the U.S. population, who will care for them? Perhaps Japan offers a possible solution.

Japan's Ministry of Economy, Trade and Industry decided that robots represent a possible solution for elder care, and it has been allocating billions of yen for developing robots for the nursing and medicine sectors of its economy. These robots are expected to serve many functions, including carrying seniors around the house, monitoring their medicine, reminding them of appointments, providing physical therapy, and interacting socially. They also can retrieve objects from high shelves, retrieve medicine and oxygen, and remind their elderly companions to eat regular meals.

The Japanese government has identified loneliness as a common affliction among its elderly because many now live alone. Toyota and IBM have invested in Israeli startup Intuition Robotics and its product, a social companion robot named ElliQ. The robot sits at a table and helps facilitate communication between its elderly companion and family by eliminating the complexity of establishing a video connection. ElliQ also tries to keep its senior companion active by personalized suggestions such as walks or specific music it can play; it also reminds a patient when his or her medicine should be taken.[36]

In fact, several companies are developing social robots for the elderly. PARO looks like a baby seal. It is known as a therapeutic companion robot and is classified in the United States as a Class Two medical device. It responds by moving its head, tail, and flippers and opening its eyes when petted.[††] Researchers have found that the elderly respond positively to this robot, but some people question the ethics of treating elderly patients like children by offering them robotic pets.

Japanese robotic researcher Hiroshi Ishiguro has developed robots known as Telenoids in senior care facilities throughout Denmark. The Danish government has purchased more than 1,000 such robots for its elder care facilities. The elderly, even those suffering from depression or dementia, respond to this strange stunted-looking creature by cradling it and treating it lovingly like a baby.[37] Ironically, some adult children have expressed concerns that the PARO might replace them in the affection of their elderly parents. In fact, medical staff have observed the elderly talking affectionately to these seal-like creatures. Despite the apparent harmlessness of such robots, there are ethical issues that must be considered.

While some robot companies have chosen to create products for seniors that look decidedly nonhuman, others have created robots that are human-like with smiling faces because such human features help the elderly feel less alone. Researchers concerned about ethics in an automated world worry that people will become less human if they give up the burden of care, the compact that ties together the human race. There is something sad at the thought of the elderly living out their last days watched over by what the hippy poet Richard Brautigan called "machines of loving grace."

––––––––––

[††] See www.pororobots.com.

While Japan faces a crisis in elder care today because of a lack of workers, the United States will face the same problem very shortly. Japan has already embraced the use of robots to handle the elderly's needs, including monitoring their medicine, their appointments, and their safety. Some elderly patients suffering from depression and even dementia apparently have responded positively when giving the opportunity to care for robotic *infants*. There are ethical issues regarding abrogating the human burden of caring for the elderly because it violates a fundamental compact that helps to keep us human. Given the changing demographics that show the elderly becoming a much more significant part of the U.S. total population, robotic workers might be required to fill the growing gap in human elder care workers.

## Robot Cleaners With Artificial Intelligence

One day I was working at home while my wife was out running an errand. I thought I heard a small voice, but I couldn't make out the words. Suddenly my wife called me to tell me that she had left our Roomba vacuum cleaner on so it could perform its work while she was out of the house. The machine had texted her that it was stuck and needed help. Startled, I found the robotic cleaner and heard it proclaiming in its tiny voice that it was "stuck on a cliff." In reality, it was stuck below a low-hanging shelf, but with its limited intelligence, it could not tell the difference. My particular model is just smart enough to find where it needs to plug itself in for recharging. Some of iRobot's (recently purchased by Amazon) other Roomba models are far more intelligent. Its 980 model, for example, uses AI to scan a room, identify obstacles, and remember the most efficient routes for cleaning. Other companies such as Brain Corporation (https://braincorp.com) now offer commercial robotic cleaners. While they cannot completely replace human cleaning crews yet, the technology is improving every year.

## Robots in Agriculture

Agriculture once was an industry that offered plenty of jobs for immigrants and other entry-level workers. The pandemic along with more restrictive immigration policies have hit this industry very hard. As a result, artificial intelligence and robots are making some headway there, even though the delicate task of handling certain types of fruit without crushing them remains an issue. Some robots, like the one that uses high-pressure water beams to cut lettuce, require humans to assist by cutting off loose leaves.[38] Vision Robotics developed these lettuce thinners by adding vision-based algorithms so that its robots can create three-dimensional maps of areas to be treated. There are even robotic pollinators to take up the slack because so many bees are dying.[39] Abundant Robotics produced a robotic apple harvester. While the robot could identify ripe fruit, pick the apples, and then place them in a bin, the pandemic forced the company to go out of business. Automato Robotics offers a tomato harvester that is far slower than a human, but can work twice as long (16 hours).[40] Perhaps that's the dirty little secret CEOs really don't want to talk about in public. Robot workers might often be slower, but they can work longer hours and don't ask for raises or benefits or join labor unions.

While driverless cars face enormous challenges when it comes to widespread deployment, driverless tractors face far less obstacles. There are challenges that remain, however, including the limitations posed by current batteries and chargers. Another limitation often not mentioned is that resistance to technological change and a concern about privacy found on many family farms.[41]

## Robots in Pharmacies

A machine called the PillPick can package and dispense prescriptions while leaving real live pharmacists to verify orders.[42] The University of California's medical complex's pharmacy in San Francisco is staffed by robots that prepare medicine for patients.[43] So, even if a pharmacy doesn't use a robotic pharmacist, using a robotic assistant to fulfill orders probably slows the hiring of additional human workers.

## Robots in the Military

Arnold Schwarzenegger's *Terminator* movies have contributed significantly to the public's view of a cold, completely rational robotic killing machine that has no emotional ties to humanity. The premise of these films is that in the not-to-distant future machines decide to exterminate humans. What is intriguing as well as disturbing is that the discussion today over the ethical and moral use of self-directed robotic weapons is no longer just theoretical. Take for example, a robotic sentry soldier, the SGR-A1 built by Samsung, currently patrolling the Korean DMZs border.

Known as a *human-on-the-loop weapon*, this sentry robot can select targets under the oversight of a human operator who can override the robot's actions. Here's the point to remember, though. When and if the robot is ever placed in fully automatic mode, it will use its built-in camera and pattern recognition software to detect an intruder and issue a verbal warning. If the intruder does not surrender, the robot will fire its machine gun.[44]

Imagine now drones that are given general instructions for identifying an enemy and freed from human control. Who is to say that the drone will not misidentify an innocent civilian as an enemy soldier? The U.S. Navy is well on its way toward implementing the use of weapons that utilize AI to make their own decisions. The Long-Range Anti-Ship Missile (LRASM) developed by Lockheed-Martin for the navy has the ability to make targeting decisions autonomously. The LRASM is designed to fly to an enemy fleet and use artificial intelligence technologies to decide which target to kill.

## The Anthropomorphic Attraction of Robot Soldiers

Robotic soldiers are already being deployed in the U.S. army, often in situations where a human soldier would be exposed to great danger. What interests some researchers is the relationship between the humans and their robotic colleagues. A University of Washington researcher has studied soldiers' emotional attachment to the robots that work alongside them. She found that the soldiers "also socialized with the robot, with acts such as assigning gender pronouns, humorously naming them, and even having memorial services if the robot was destroyed."[45] Another researcher reported how a soldier responded when a robot he knew was blown up as if he had lost a fellow soldier.[46]

The point to be made is that soldiers think of their robotic colleagues as human to some degree. Does that make them more comfortable in freeing these robots from human constraints on the battlefield and assuming they will exercise the same degree of human restraint when it comes to killing innocent people?

The other aspect of robotic soldiers is that the volunteer army traditionally has been a way for noncollege-educated young people to take advantage of the military's educational programs to move up to middle-class status. The more robotic soldiers become a standard part of the military, the fewer opportunities there will be for young people to learn technical skills while earning a salary.

## Corporations Choose Profits Over People

While many companies justify replacing human workers with robots by arguing that they have to protect their bottom line, others have found other ways to rationalize their preference for robots over humans. One company's CEO argued that replacing humans enabled it to move 90 percent of its manufacturing back to the United States, a decision it described as *patriotic capitalism* and a way to keep America strong.[47] No matter the rationalization, companies that replace humans with robots without worrying about the long-term impact on society of massive unemployment are contributing to a problem that could prove very difficult to solve in the future as robots become more capable and the number of employment options for human workers begins to markedly decline.

## Careers in Robotics

There's a scene in the movie *The Graduate* when a family friend whispers one word, *plastics*, to Dustin Hoffman's character to convey the ideal career choice in the 1960s. Today, the career advice probably would be *robotics* if not *artificial intelligence*. While there are plenty of entry-level positions, more senior positions require graduate education. Robots are proliferating in many different industries. Health care professionals are likely to encounter robotic surgeons, while driverless cars and warehouse robots are becoming much more common. Robotics encompasses many different disciplines, including artificial intelligence, software development, and engineering. LearnRobotics.org is a website that provides a lot of valuable information on different career paths. There are a number of different career paths, depending on people's interests. There are mechanical and electrical engineering tracks as well as software and user interface paths. Another way to view the various career paths is to categorize them as working on the way robots think, the way they move and process the world around them, and the way they communicate with humans.

## Majors and Centers of Robotics Instruction

Until recently, it was not possible to earn an undergraduate degree in robotics. Recently, Florida International University became the first university to offer a BS degree in robotics. Today, most students interested in a career in robotics will earn their undergraduate degrees in such areas as computer science, engineering, and neuroscience. The major centers of instruction at the graduate level include Carnegie Mellon, Cornell, Harvard, MIT, Stanford, Michigan, Georgia Institute of Technology, University of Washington, USC, UCLA, and UC Berkley. These schools do offer undergraduate courses that can prepare students for graduate work in robotics.

## Short-Term Learning Opportunities in Robotics

There are countless online robotics courses available, many of which are free or very inexpensive. Udemy, edX, and Coursera offer a wide array of courses, and Classcentral.com lists more than 100 free online courses. Stanford's engineering department offers a robotics class online, while MIT has an extensive 10-week program titled MIT XPro Robotics Essentials ($2,600) that requires 8 to 10 hours per week to earn a certificate in designing and building robot systems.

## Validating Knowledge of Robotics for Those Already in Careers

For those people who already are in the workforce and would love to find a way to transition to a job that includes robotics, the best way remains opting for one of the many online certificate programs. MIT's program is pricey, but the MIT name on the certificate might go a long way to validate knowledge. The hardest part of learning about robotics without going back to school is acquiring the hands-on knowledge.

# CHAPTER 4

# 3D and 4D Printing

While the traditional way to manufacture something using a mold is to start with a block of some kind of material and then carve out the item, 3D printing falls under the category of additive manufacturing. That means a 3D printer manufactures an item by *printing* a thin layer composed of plastic or other materials and then repeating the process over and over until it creates a three-dimensional object. The printer follows a set of instructions created with a computer-assisted drawing program.

3D printers have been around since the 1980s in one form or another, but it is only within the past few years that the technology has improved to the point that they are attracting more than amateurs called *makers*. Just when this technology is beginning to accelerate, scientists at MIT have been experimenting with 4D printers. A 4D printer is a 3D printer that prints using special materials that alter their shape and function over time based on external stimuli such as light, heat, or electricity. Imagine, for example, an item that ships flat but can be stimulated to form a far different shape. A water valve could be *printed* using material that expands when hot water flows and contracts when cold water flows. The possibilities are endless, but practical applications of this technology are still too far in the future to consider for now in terms of their impact on jobs gained or lost, so this chapter will focus on the impact of 3D printer technology.

## The Promise of 3D Printer Technology

3D printing does have the potential to change the entire economic order. China dominates manufacturing today because of its cheap labor. Imagine new technology that turned that advantage into a disadvantage. Imagine if people could create their own customized goods locally, either in their homes or in nearby printing centers. Finally, imagine if local automobile dealers printed out most of their models and customized them for local tastes.

The value proposition would be that a company would no longer need to rely on a long supply line that included having goods travel on enormous cargo ships and dealing with the logistics of having these goods trucked or delivered by rail to warehouses and then finally to local dealers.

Imagine the health care field turned upside down because organ donation would no longer be necessary because organs could be printed out using specialized 3D printers. Rather than have to buy new products when spare parts become impossible to find, people could download designs for spare parts and then print out the parts themselves. Retail clothing stores would offer customized printing of designs, while people living in colonies on other planets would print out their own dwellings rather than carry heavy construction materials into space. Now that we've imagined the possibilities, let's look at where the technology is right now in several key industries. The recurring theme throughout my comments on the various industry uses of 3D printing is its potential. While so much has been accomplished within the past few years, this technology is still emerging, although it is already clear that its eventual impact on jobs will be substantial.

## 3D Printers in the Medical and Dentistry Industries

3D printers have dramatically cut the cost of a number of dental procedures. A number of companies, including Sprintray (www.sprintray .com), now offer 3D printers that can print dental crowns, speeding up the procedure from what used to take up to three weeks to around 10 minutes. Some of these printers print a material called Zirconia, a substance even stronger than the porcelain used in crowns produced the traditional way. 3D printers can even print jaws. In 2012, doctors at the University of Hasselt BIOMED Research Institute in Belgium replaced an 83-year-old woman's lower jaw with one created by a 3D printer using titanium powder.[1]

Creating prosthetics is also a far less expensive process when a 3D printer prints them. Unlimited Tomorrow (www.unlimitedtomorrow .com) uses a process in which a candidate for a new limb fills out a questionnaire, scans the area where the limb will go, and submits the information to the company. It points out on its website that it can produce a prosthetic arm for around $8,000, compared to the $20,000 to $80,000 required using traditional methods. Figure 4.1 displays a prosthetic hand the company produced on a 3D printer. PVA Med (www .pvamed.net) is another provider offering a turnkey replacement limb service that includes the socket design and fabrication process using a 3D scanner and a 3D printer.

The point to make here is that the cost savings and timesaving clearly will have a ripple impact on the prosthetics industry. Small, agile companies with trained 3D printer computer-assisted design (CAD) designers will be able to grow rapidly, while more traditional prosthetic manufacturers will lose customers. That change will impact the traditional supply chain for these products as well as sales channels. Technical trainers will be needed to help salespeople acquire the ability to explain 3D printer technology.

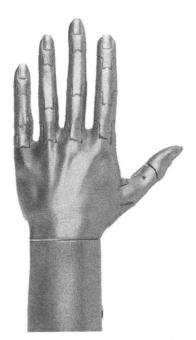

*Figure 4.1  A prosthetic hand 3D printed by Unlimited Tomorrow*

Photo by Unlimited Tomorrow www.unlimitedtomorrow.com.

## Replacement Organs

The holy grail of 3D printer medical applications is the ability to create functional replacement organs by *printing* them using bio ink, a substance usually composed of cells and a gel-like substance used to create a 3D scaffolding.[2] While it has long been possible to *print* an organ, the problem has been creating an organ that contains the complex network of blood vessels necessary to keep that organ alive. Scientists are close to achieving that goal. As far as organ tissue goes, Organovo can now *print* human liver tissue that can be used by patients waiting to receive human liver transplants. Researchers at Newcastle University have produced a proof-of-concept 3D printed cornea, a step closer to printing that organ for people needing a replacement. The actual printing took less than 10 minutes.[3]

The ripple impact of 3D printing on the organ replacement field will create new jobs. Besides a growing need for 3D printer technicians, a new type of supply chain will need to be created. Rather than the occasional sight of a doctor rushing into a hospital clutching an ice chest containing a recently removed organ to be used for a transplant operation, it likely will be a far more common sight to observe employees of companies that print organs delivering them as needed. This new industry will require new insurance brokers as well as a new legal specialization to handle cases involving 3D printed organs. On the other hand, employees of kidney dilation centers will find far less demand for their services. Manufacturers of ventricular assist devices and replacement valves will also see their sales fall.

## 3D Printing in Construction

It is possible to *print* an entire house because large, specialized 3D printers now have the ability to *print* concrete. A 2,700-square-foot home in Dubai was printed in 2016.[4] When the COVID-19 virus first appeared in China, the government needed more coronavirus quarantine rooms. The Shanghai firm Winsun Building Technique Company developed a printer that can produce 15 such rooms a day for around $4,000. Each room is large enough to hold two beds.[5] U.S. builders such as ICON (iconbuild .com) are using 3D printers to create entire housing tracts.

Anything an architect can imagine can be incorporated into a CAD design and then printed out. One marketing manager pointed to a 60 percent reduction in time on site and an 80 percent savings on labor costs when a commercial building is printed rather than constructed.[6] So, if that's the case, why doesn't 3D printing dominate the construction industry?

The answer is that it might in the near future, but there are obstacles that still need to be overcome, including the lack of adequate regulations, the threat of legal liability for employee accidents, and the lack of technically educated workers and trainers. Ironically, construction has long been a field that attracted immigrants and young people looking for jobs that did not require extensive education and experience. Yet, those are precisely the workers who ultimately could be displaced when 3D printing becomes far more common in construction. As an example, the McKinsey consulting firm estimates a 24 percent decrease in jobs for construction crane and tower operators by 2030.[7]

At the same time, though, demand for CAD designers, trainers, and 3D technicians will expand. There will also be a demand for specialized value-added resellers who focus on construction-specific 3D printing applications, can warehouse the products, and then train construction workers in their use. Because of the enormous numbers of laborers injured each year in construction accidents, there will also be opportunities for lawyers and insurance people who specialize in construction-related 3D printer incidents.

One important fact to keep in mind, though, is that while construction workers of the future will need to be 3D printer-savvy, that will not necessarily require a college degree. More and more high schools and libraries are offering free 3D printer training. The 3D printer field has not codified to the point that an employee needs a degree in additive manufacturing, unless the career goal is to be an engineer.

## 3D Printing in Manufacturing

At its present stage of development, 3D printing does not lend itself to the massive production of products we usually think of when we think of large-scale manufacturing operations. While enthusiasts have actually

3D printed a car, the technology as a proof-of-concept is not cost-effective enough to replace existing auto plants. On the other hand, though, 3D printer technology is ideal for small runs of customized objects. The creation of prototypes is one area where 3D printing excels because the emphasis is on speed and customization. No two prototypes are the same.

Craftsmen have been using 3D printers to produce customizable jewelry. Imagine the near future when someone needs a replacement part, whether for a home appliance or even for an automobile. Rather than pay for a physical warehouse for thousands of items or even a long supply line that stretches from wholesalers to retail part dealers, a company might answer a customer request after the payment of a fee with a CAD file that will enable that customer to *print* that part at home or go to a neighborhood specialized printing center.

The ripples that 3D printing in the manufacturing sector will cause in its labor market will be profound. While some warehouse jobs will be lost, print centers will spring up with a demand for knowledgeable 3D printing workers. Specialized companies will spring up to provide product-specific media for 3D printer owners. People's homes will become manufacturing operations for crafts that don't lend themselves to factory production but could provide lucrative income for home workers. A print-on-demand model means that such a home operation would require little storage. As this manufacturing area grows, it will create jobs for people in companies that will spring up to provide what 3D home printing jobs require, just as the recent coronavirus restrictions that kept so many employees working from home created a new niche market for companies specializing in making work from home more efficient and enjoyable.

## 3D Printing in Retail

Just as FedEx and UPS stores sprung up to provide printing, mailing, and copying neighborhood services, imagine 3D printer centers that will utilize more expensive high-speed 3D printers. A customer will compare the time savings of printing there rather than printing at home on a slow but inexpensive printer and head out the door. Just as an embryonic personal computer industry created the necessity of neighborhood computer stores to provide the *hand-holding* nontechnical customers required to become comfortable with their purchases, 3D printer stores could also spring up to go along with those stores offering print services. The printer stores would also sell accessories and offer classes, thus creating employment opportunities for salespeople and trainers as well as CAD designers.

## 3D Printers in the Clothing Industry

3D printing could have an enormous impact on the clothing industry. As a proof-of-concept, there have been fashion shows where designers used 3D printers to create dresses costing thousands of dollars. Among the ideas under development right now are 3D printers that will be able to take old clothes and then use that material to create and print completely new clothes. Clothing manufacturers could sell customers special cartridges that could then be used to print designer clothes.[8]

Retail clothing salespeople would not be as necessary when people could customize pictures of clothing to their exact measurements, observe how they look in three-dimensional holograms, and then *print* the clothing at home.

## 3D Printer Education Opportunities

3D printing classes are becoming common in high schools and even in some elementary schools. Libraries are offering classes as well. This demand for teachers and trainers will accelerate with the growth of the 3D printer industry. There are already a number of ways to earn certificates to show mastery of the technology. Skills, rather than formal degrees, will be preferable for the next several years, much the same way trainers when the personal computer industry was new were hired based on their familiarity with computer technology since formal degrees in computer science were still so rare.

## Future 3D Printer Applications

For readers with most of their careers still in the future, 3D printing will have a significant impact depending on their industry. Take the pharmaceutical industry as an example. It is conceivable that by 2050, a doctor's prescription will enable a patient to unlock the CAD design for printing that prescription on a home 3D printer. Sounds impossible? Consider that specialized 3D printers are already beginning to print organs as well as food and even meat. The result would be less need for pharmacists and pharmacist technicians/customer support people. There is already serious consideration for including 3D printers on the ships traveling to Mars to establish a Martian colony. These printers could print replacement parts, food, and, eventually medicine.

Homes will spring up rapidly and cost far less because specialized printers can print out the structures and even include the plumbing and electrical components inside the walls they print. Current builders like ICON already incorporate environmentally friendly features into the homes they print. In the future, as climate change becomes accepted as perhaps the major challenge to humanity, 3D printing will assume a much more significant role in construction. Figure 4.2 lists some of the future jobs 3D printing will create.

Similarly, there will be far less demand for people in commercial real estate because there will be less demand for warehouses as more companies turn to a business model that enables customers to print their products at home or send designs to print centers. One prime example is toy manufacturing. Fewer people will rush to stores to buy their toys, and so those stores will order fewer toys from distributors. The political and economic impacts could be enormous as trade with China could decrease considerably.

In fact, a more 3D printing technology would change so many business models that it would justify designating it a disruptive technology.

- 3D printing center staff
- 3D organ printing technician
- 3D printer food specialist
- 3D printing software developer
- 3D printer food QC specialist
- 3D printing construction specialist
- 3D printing trainer
- 3D printing food marketing specialist
- 3D printing prosthetics specialist
- 3D printing clothing specialist

*Figure 4.2 Some Future 3D Printing Jobs*

Take Amazon as an example. It uses a model that requires vast warehouses to store products close enough to customers to justify them paying for prime membership so that they can receive items in two days shipped free. Imagine how many of these products could be printed at home. Larger 3D printers will be able to print furniture. In fact, IKEA could e-mail plans and assembly instructions to customers so that they could print the furniture at home. When 4D printers become common, IKEA could have customers print out a flattened piece of furniture that, when subjected to heat or electrical stimuli, could pop out into its final shape.

Disruptive technology disrupts the *status quo* and results in temporary dislocation until society adjusts. 3D printing will certainly impact a number of jobs in a negative way, including the following: transportation and delivery of products, warehouse workers, commercial real estate brokers and salespeople, retail salespeople, and construction laborers.

On the other hand, 3D printing will create jobs for salespeople, designers, trainers, technicians, customer service people, legal and insurance 3D printer specialists, and so on. Workers will be needed to maintain and repair equipment, as well as produce the increasing numbers of materials used by the printers. It will create millions of cottage industries for people who want to create items and then sell them over the Internet. This latter category is critical because these products will likely fall into niche market segments that are too narrow to warrant the use of robots or artificial intelligence, and so they will serve as a safe harbor for human workers.

## Roadblocks to 3D Printer Technology Reaching Its Full Potential

There are several roadblocks that still need to be overcome for 3D printing to reach its full potential. While the American Society of Testing and Materials (ASTM) F42 Committee has made significant progress in developing standards in various areas, such as metal powders and aerospace material specifications, its task is far from finished. Quality control is also an issue because there is still too much variance in the items printed. Vendors are currently developing new types of materials for printing that will be necessary to create new markets. Examples include new types of strong but light metal for the aerospace industry, food products, and fabrics. There is also the problem of cost, which will be solved eventually as the volume of 3D printers increases and the price per unit decreases.

## A Likely Timeline for Widespread Adoption

It is likely that standards will be in place, and more key materials will be available by 2030. While 3D printing will not be ideal for every small manufacturing job, it is likely that this technology's share of manufacturing dollars will increase from less than one percent to around 15 percent by 2035. By 2030, high-school graduates should be well trained in 3D printer technology, and most community colleges will be offering advanced classes in this technology. Those trends will spur growth because there will no longer be a shortage of trainers and technicians.*

## Careers in 3D and 4D Printing

Careers in 3D and 4D printing will cut across a number of different industries. One area primed to explode is organ and prosthetic printing. Construction, manufacturing, education, and law are other areas likely to add 3D and 4D printer personnel. There also are likely to be opportunities for people with business backgrounds and knowledge of 3D and 4D printing to establish services businesses.

## Majors and Centers of Instruction

3D and 4D printing fall under the category of additive manufacturing as well as the more general area of materials science. The major learning centers for additive manufacturing generally focus on graduate degrees. Undergraduate degrees in engineering as well as in computer-aided manufacturing and design prepare students for entry-level positions as well as qualify them for pursuing graduate programs. Those students who want to prepare themselves for biological applications of 3D printing should

---

* See M. Patch. January 23, 2020. "100 Printing Experts Predict the Future of 3D Printing in 2030." 3Dprintingindustry.com (accessed April 20, 2022).

consider a biology major, while those interested in legal applications of 3D printing should consider a prelaw major while also learning as much as they can about 3D printer technology and software. Major centers of learning often mentioned include MIT, Purdue, Penn State, Carnegie Mellon, and Ohio State.

## Short-Term 3D Printing Learning Opportunities

Coursera offers over 20 additive manufacturing courses online. In fact, there are a number of 3D printing courses available online. University extension departments offer many of these programs. The University of California's San Diego (UCSD) and Irvine (UCI) campuses have offered courses and certificate programs. The key, though, is acquiring hands-on experience. Many public libraries offer courses in 3D printing, including using computer-assisted design (CAD) software. It is also now possible to purchase inexpensive 3D printers to gain hands-on experience. For self-learners, there are plenty of books available to help learn 3D software and hardware.

## Validating Knowledge for Those Already in Careers

The beauty of this field is that it is still so new that employers do not expect undergraduate degrees in this area. That's why certificate programs as well as hands-on experience are so valuable when it comes to validating the knowledge required for an entry-level position. SME.org offers a certification program in additive manufacturing. Don't overlook the 3D printer certification programs available at a number of community colleges. As an example, Lackawanna Community College (Lackawanna .edu) offers three different levels of certificates in 3D printing.

# CHAPTER 5

# Blockchain and Cryptocurrencies

Blockchain and Bitcoin can be traced back to 2009 when someone using the pseudonym Satoshi Nakamoto published the documentation for Bitcoin, a cryptocurrency that used a blockchain to keep track of its transactions. The blockchain consists of blocks of data on an ever-increasing number of distributed servers that communicate with each other in a peer-to-peer network with no single entity in control. The blockchain Nakamoto proposed is public and encrypted.

Because each block of the long blockchain contains the same transactional information, it is virtually impossible to alter an entry. Nakamoto also set a limit of 21 million Bitcoins with a proviso that made *mining* Bitcoins more difficult as the number still remaining becomes smaller. Keep in mind that there are other blockchains that support other cryptocurrencies such as Ethereum.

## Blockchain Accounting and Other Business Applications

When discussing the impact of emerging technologies on careers in the near future, blockchain and cryptocurrencies must be viewed as intertwined from a technological perspective but distinctly different when it comes to their impact on jobs. While cryptocurrency will create a number of new job categories, blockchain technology on its own will have an enormous impact on many industries and create all kinds of new jobs.

By its very nature, blockchain technology offers a way to track transactions that is safe, secure, and cost-effective. Take musicians, for example, a blockchain can track intellectual property usage and royalties due. A blockchain can also maintain a detailed record of items in a supply chain. If a batch of spinach turns out to contain E. coli, it becomes easy for the grocery chain at the end of the supply chain to quickly locate where the bad packages are located. Insurance companies will be able to cut fraud by determining who is the rightful owner of an insurance policy. Analysts have pointed to Medicare fraud as one area where a blockchain could cut fraud, but another area is the sale of expensive items. A blockchain could maintain the chain of ownership for items such as diamonds and works of art and cut fraud.

## Blockchains Will Generate Jobs

In the short run, blockchain technology will generate an enormous number of jobs because it will create entirely new job categories that require some knowledge of how a blockchain can be created and maintained. Of course, a number of jobs generated will fall into the technical category as companies will need to fill programming, engineering, security, and design positions. Still, companies will also need to hire accountants, marketing people, and technical writers with a knowledge of how blockchains work. A quick search of *blockchain* jobs at the cryptocurrencyjobs.co website found blockchain marketing managers, operations managers, business development staff, product analysts, technical writers, investment analysts, and so on. In other words, many companies are now finding that they need to staff up in all areas where blockchain will impact their businesses.

## Cryptocurrency Will Also Create Jobs

Up until the recent market fall, cryptocurrency companies were also in high growth mode. This market reached a peak of over $3 trillion dollars.[1] In addition to crypto brokers, technical writers, researchers, security personnel, social media writers, the industry requires engineers, programmers, product managers, and so on. The impact of cryptocurrency on financial markets has created openings for investment analysts, portfolio managers, consultants, and brokers. Retailers have to hire people who can make it possible for them to handle cryptocurrency transactions. A number of companies have large numbers of *unbanked* customers now or

- Smart contract lawyer
- Cryptocurrency broker
- Cryptocurrency financial advisor
- Blockchain accounting specialist
- Blockchain engineer
- Blockchain programmer
- Blockchain cybersecurity specialist
- Blockchain real estate specialist
- Blockchain business developer

*Figure 5.1 Some future blockchain and cryptocurrency jobs*

would like to add them in the future. That group is among the earliest adopters of cryptocurrency in part because it makes it easy and inexpensive for them to send funds to family living overseas. As they are already comfortable using cryptocurrency, companies will want to make it possible for them to handle cryptocurrency transactions. Figure 5.1 displays some future blockchain- and cryptocurrency-related jobs.

## Current Obstacles to Even More Explosive Growth

There are a number of obstacles today that prevent even more explosive growth of blockchains and cryptocurrencies. One problem is a lack of trained personnel. Because blockchain technology is so new, it is not something widely taught in colleges. That creates an opportunity for people willing to take any one of several certificate programs available through online programs as well as *bootcamps* that provide intensive training in a short period of time. A second issue is the uncertainty over how much regulation governments will impose. A third issue is confusion over the proliferation of thousands of different coins or *tokens* on cryptocurrencies that compete with Bitcoin and Ethereum. The effect in some cases for people new to this field is analysis paralysis.

Finally, there are also some technical issues that are in the process of being solved but still remain obstacles today. One is the transaction time required for a Bitcoin transaction to ripple through its enormous blockchain. Some services charge fees to accelerate the process. Another issue right now is the huge fluctuation in the price of cryptocurrencies. The wild swings in value are an obstacle to more conservative investors entering this field. Also, a number of stories in the media have focused on criminals using cryptocurrencies as well as stories of people losing their fortunes because they lost the passwords to their digital wallets.

While some countries such as Vietnam have banned cryptocurrencies, El Salvador has made Bitcoin its official currency along with the U.S. dollar. The U.S. government officials have been mulling regulations while facing support for strict regulations from banks that see cryptocurrencies as competition and opposition against excessive regulation from a wide range of supporters. The lack of government regulation and the concern over what kind of regulation is in the future remains a very serious obstacle to explosive growth of blockchains and cryptocurrencies. Today, the IRS treats cryptocurrency as property, meaning that when someone buys, sells, or exchanges it, this counts as a taxable event and results in either a capital gain or loss. This complicates the use of cryptocurrencies enormously. When someone earns income from cryptocurrency activities, this is taxed as ordinary income.

## Blockchain and Cryptocurrency Creates Winners and Losers

The banking industry potentially has the most to lose if cryptocurrency and blockchain technology grows exponentially. It would lose several lucrative sources of income, including transaction fees, wire transfer fees, and loan fees. Cryptocurrency will offer virtually free alternatives to the first two revenue streams while blockchain technology's ability to create peer-to-peer relationships between people willing to lend money and those people seeking loans will hurt banks' revenue from loans. In fact, some companies are working on ways for blockchain technology to establish credit evaluations that will even eliminate the need to use the three major credit evaluation companies. So, people in the banking industry who work in the areas threatened by this new technology will likely find their jobs going away. Companies like Western Union that charge exorbitant fees for transferring money for the *unbanked* also will be hurt by the growing acceptance of cryptocurrency.

Banking is not the only industry blockchain will impact. Imagine the number of people working in insurance fraud departments. Once that industry embraces blockchains, many of their jobs will go away because the blockchain will clearly establish the rightful owner of the insurance policy because it is impossible to forge all the copies of an entry in a blockchain. The federal government and a number of health insurance companies are researching blockchain technology now. Imagine if all of a person's health information and all related transactions, including drug prescriptions, could be encrypted securely and tracked. Fewer people would be required to maintain health records, and doctors who prescribe thousands of opioids would be easily identified. As I mentioned earlier in the chapter, Medicare fraud would be reduced significantly, but that also might mean fewer investigators needed to search through thousands of files.

Blockchain and cryptocurrency also will spur growth in some industries. In the previous chapter, we looked at the enormous numbers of craftspeople who could start their own businesses using 3D printers. Imagine if these people could put their sales transactions onto a blockchain that would ensure that they get paid for their work because the indelible record of these transactions would serve as proof they shipped their merchandise.

## Blockchain Could Impact the Legal Field

Blockchain technology permits what is called a *smart contract*. This means that software can be added to the blockchain that creates a series of conditions that must be met for certain actions to take place. In Arizona, parties now can create enforceable legal agreements through smart contracts.* This ruling could hurt lawyers who specialize in entertainment law. Smart contracts on a blockchain could make it possible for musicians and other creative types to ensure they receive royalties on every purchase of their products. As fraud would be far more difficult because of the unchangeable blockchain records, there should be far less litigation required.

---

* See "The Future of Blockchain Technology in 2022." January 7, 2022. getsmarter.com. www.getsmarter.com/blog/market-trends/the-future-of-block-chain-technology-in-2022/ (accessed April 26, 2022).

## Future Real Estate Sales Could Eliminate the Middle Man

Realtors in the future might find buyers and sellers bypassing them via a smart contract on a blockchain. Fewer people doing title searches might also be required because blockchains could make it easy to determine if a title is valid.

## Used Car Purchases Could Be Far Easier

Imagine if a car's complete maintenance and accident histories were on a blockchain. No longer would potential buyers have to accept an owner or a salesperson's word that a car was in good shape. In fact, blockchain technology would make it much easier for people to sell their cars and other products to each other without a salesperson in the middle of the transaction.

## Online Games and Virtual Reality Will Spur the Growth of Cryptocurrencies

Play-to-earn (P2E) game companies sell games where gamers earn cryptocurrency. Axie Infinity is an example of a popular P2E crypto game. Its own in-game currency can be converted into cash, and it also uses another token known as the Axie Infinity Token. In fact, a survey of online gamers revealed that around 75 percent of them want to exchange their virtual assets for currency they can take to other platforms to buy and sell items.[†] How big is this market? Newzoo's Analytics Platforms estimates that the online game market will surpass $200 billion by 2023.[‡]

Similarly, Meta (formally Facebook) is betting heavily that people visiting the metaverse will want to buy virtual reality objects. They also most likely will pay for these items with cryptocurrency. This market is already a lot larger than most outsiders realize. As of June 1, 2022, the *Cryptoslate*

---

[†] "Is Cryptocurrency the Future of Online Gaming?" April 19, 2022. dailygazette .com. https://dailygazette.com/is-cryptocurrency-the-future-of-online-gaming/ (accessed April 26, 2022).

[‡] Ibid.

*.com* website estimated the market cap for virtual reality cryptocurrency, tokens, and coins at $2.21 billion dollars.

## Momentum for the Growth of Blockchain and Cryptocurrencies

There are a number of reasons to believe that the future is rosy for blockchain technology as well as for cryptocurrency. Blockchain has the advantage of solving real business problems and being easy to justify because of cost savings through the reduction of fraud. Advocates of cryptocurrency point out that that governments have the ability to manipulate their currencies by artificially propping up their value. They also can print more money to cover deficit spending and thus create inflation. As there is a finite number of Bitcoins that can be mined (21 million), it is not subject to the type of inflation fiat (government controlled and created) currencies face as there is no central authority that can *print* more Bitcoins.

## Likely Timeline for Growth

Blockchain and cryptocurrency already have attracted early adopters. Much like the wild-west environment that characterized the early growth stage of the Internet, investors have been quick to fund startups because they feared being left behind of the *next big thing*. Fortune 500 companies have begun hiring staff to build blockchains because this technology offers improved efficiency and significant cost savings. Cryptocurrencies are also growing to the point that leading mutual fund managers have been creating new offerings for investors who want to dip their toes in this market while still playing it safe.

The period 2021–2022 saw a major dip in cryptocurrencies as investors fled to what they considered more secure investments. Most industry experts see Bitcoin and other cryptocurrencies rebounding in the future much as they have in the past. In 2022, the industry saw major technical improvements to blockchain technology with the creation of an Ethereum 2.0 specification that should make it easier to scale very large blockchains. Assuming the U.S. government develops reasonable regulations for managing cryptocurrencies, growth should accelerate over the next decade. During this period, blockchain and cryptocurrencies will create far more jobs than they will eliminate. The Gartner Group characterizes 2018–2021 as the *irrational exuberance* stage for blockchain, followed by large-scale investments and many successful models (2022–2026), and finally, a third phase of successful global expansion (2027–2030).[2]

## Careers in Blockchain and Cryptocurrencies

Careers in blockchain and cryptocurrency look very promising at this point because these are such new technologies that there is a severe shortage of people who are knowledgeable. Careers can take many different forms. Blockchain accounting or law are two new areas, but certainly, blockchain will generate career opportunities in transportation and logistics, insurance, and real estate, while cryptocurrency will offer its own career paths, including security, software, brokerage, investment, sales, and so on.

## Majors and Centers of Instruction

Blockchain and cryptocurrency are new technologies, and most universities have not caught up yet to the point that they offer full majors. Students should consider majors such as business administration, finance, and accounting. Those interested in the technical side might want to major in computer science, software engineering, or even cybersecurity, if such a major is available.

## Short-Term Learning Opportunities

There is a wealth of online courses and certifications, many free or very inexpensive. Coursera.org has a number of blockchain and cryptocurrency courses and certifications. The University of Buffalo, as an example, offers a four-course certification in blockchain, while Princeton offers both blockchain and cryptocurrency courses. edX.org offers a program from UC Berkeley, while Udemy.com also offers classes. MIT Sloan's Executive management program also offers an online program. Another way of learning about the field is to attend a trade show on blockchain and/or cryptocurrency.

## Validating Knowledge for Those Already in Careers

For those people already working who would like to validate their knowledge, the certificate programs are ideal because they are online and can be taken without having to leave a job. 101 Blockchains (101blockchains .com) offers a program to become a certified enterprise blockchain professional. There also are intensive *bootcamps* that are intensive but relatively short term. Among the many schools offering such programs are Pepperdine, Arizona State, Columbia, Cornell, University of Chicago, and UC Berkeley.

# CHAPTER 6

# Improved Green Technologies Will Create Millions of Jobs

*Green technologies* refer to technologies that contribute to sustaining or restoring the environment. Rather than limiting itself to one industry, these technologies will impact virtually all major industries from the auto industry where electric cars are on the rise, thanks to new batteries that offer greater range, to construction where smart buildings are being built that conserve natural resources while minimizing energy usage. What is clear already is that while new industries and consequently new categories of jobs will spring up to address needs created by environmental regulations, accountants, project managers, marketing managers, salespeople, and others without environmental job titles will be needed to handle environmental issues. Accountants, as an example, will find increasing demand for their services if they have the knowledge required to deal with carbon credits, while salespeople selling the benefits of energy derived from solar or wind power will need to understand the basics of those technologies. More lawyers will be attracted to the field of environmental law, while the blizzard of new regulations will create opportunities for administrators to ensure that these requirements are being met. Many white-collar workers will be able to enhance their credentials and increase their value to employers by adding certificates in green areas to their resumes without having to leave work to back to school full time.

Environmental awareness can be traced in part back to 1969 when an astronaut's photograph of the Earth from space (known as Earthrise) helped people realize the fragility of this planet. Also, people were moved by a 1971 television advertisement that featured an Indian paddling a canoe and shedding a tear as he sees how people have polluted the river and land that once were so pristine. Still, it is only within the past decade that technological advances have made it practical and cost-effective for a number of industries to begin to move toward producing sustainable products.

## Green Energy on the Rise

The growth of green energy over the past five years had been very dramatic. The Department of Energy reported that in 2020, over three million Americans were employed by the clean energy sector, while in 2019, traditional fossil fuels sectors employed 1.2 million Americans.[1] The share of the energy market figures for 2020 reveal that renewable energy from wind, solar, hydroelectric, and geothermal accounted for 21 percent of all the electricity generated in the U.S. Coal represented 19 percent, while nuclear (20 percent) and natural gas (40 percent) comprised the rest.[2]

## Solar Energy Jobs

Silicon solar cells were invented at Bell Labs, yet China now dominates the manufacturing of solar silicon. China has designated green technology as one of the key industries it plans to dominate. Its current pre-eminence in this area is because a few years ago, it dumped enormous numbers of these items below cost in this country. When American solar chip manufacturers complained, the U.S. government raised duties on Chinese products and then China reciprocated. The result was that virtually, all the American manufacturers of solar energy silicon went out of business. That trend is beginning to change now primarily because of the U.S. government's realization of just how dangerous it is to rely on such a long supply chain for critical products. Also, the Biden administration states that it wanted to rebuild its domestic solar industry to create more jobs in this country. One way of building chip manufacturing capacity here is to pass a solar manufacturing rebate law that is under discussion.[3] There are efforts now to revive manufacturing silicon for solar energy in this country. States are starting to stimulate demand for solar panels. In fact, California now requires solar panels on all new home construction. The U.S. Government's Bureau of Labor Statistics forecast in 2022 that the number of photovoltaic installers would grow by over six million from 2020 to 2030, a 52.2 percent employment change.*

## Wind Energy Jobs

The Global Wind Energy Council forecasts 3.3 million wind energy jobs within the next five years.[4] In fact, wind energy is a focus of the Biden administration. It wants to expand its offshore wind capacity to 30 gigawatts by 2030 in an effort to generate jobs. Note that the current offshore wind facility built in 2016 only generates 30 megawatts. The government estimates that this increase in offshore wind capacity will lead to 44,000 jobs in this sector as well an additional 33,000 jobs in other related roles by 2030.[5] The U.S. Bureau of Labor Statistics rates wind turbine service technicians as the fastest growing job in the United States between 2020 and 2030, with a projected growth from 6.9 million to 11.7 million workers, a percent increase of 68 percent.[†] Improved wind energy technology is spurring this growth, including longer and lighter rotor blades with better design to take advantage of high winds.

## Geothermal Job Potential Is Enormous

Geothermal energy technology leverages the enormous heat found at the Earth's core to heat water into steam and then uses it to turn a turbine and generate electricity. This type of energy has been limited due to cost and complexity. That might all be changing now. There are currently 64 geothermal plants in the United States because they require a location that meets several requirements. There are plans to double that number. Enhanced geothermal technology eliminates the need to find locations where water is present along with heat. Instead, pressurized water is pushed through the rocks and heated. The problem is a political one because the technique technically is fracking, an approach that many people, especially environmentalists, fear will pollute water supplies.

---

* "Fastest Growing Occupations." April 19, 2022. bls.gov. www.bls.gov/emp/tables/fastest-growing-occupations.htm (accessed April 28, 2022).
† Ibid.

The geothermal industry insists that is not the case. The Department of Energy forecasts that the ability to generate geothermal energy using this new approach could generate five times the current energy capacity in the United States.[6] The U.S. Department of Energy announced in 2022 that it would provide $20 million dollars to develop enhanced drilling procedures as drilling represents over half of the expense of developing a new geothermal site. While the current employment in this industry is small, it is attracting the attention of oil and gas companies such as Halliburton because it is a natural fit in terms of the similarity of tasks required, including drilling. While there is no way that oil and gas companies will be able to repurpose all its workers for geothermal work, it is an area that offers future promise of absorbing some of these people.[7]

## Green Construction Will Create New Jobs

Green construction focuses on creating buildings that are energy efficient. This field creates jobs for architects, project managers, and suppliers of these materials as well as several other related jobs. Leadership in Energy and Design (LEED) is a third-party building certification program that provides training in the design, construction, and operation of energy-efficient buildings. State regulations are propelling the growth of green buildings. California's Energy Efficiency Strategic Plan from 2008 established 2030 as a target date for 50 percent of commercial building retrofits and all new commercial constructions to be energy efficient.[8]

## Electric Vehicles' Mixed Impact on Jobs

President Biden has set a goal that electric cars represent half of all new automobiles sold in the United States in 2030. There is no question that regulations as well as improved battery technology providing greater range will drive increased sales. The issue is whether the trend toward electric cars will have jobs. Today, the vehicle manufacturing sector, including suppliers, generates around a million jobs.[9] The real problem from a jobs perspective is that electric cars require at least 30 percent fewer parts. That means no need for services like oil changes, carburetor repair, and so on. The entire gasoline-powered automobile industry is a complex ecosystem that includes parts manufacturers, distributors, and salespeople as well as auto dealers, gas station personnel, and so on. Analysis by the Economic Policy Institute forecasts a loss of 75,000 jobs by 2030 if there is no government intervention with subsidies and an increase of 100,000 jobs if the government requires a higher percentage of electric vehicle parts be manufactured domestically.[10] Auto dealers could lose as much as 40 percent of their revenue[11] because an analysis of electric vehicles revealed that they have fewer parts and require far less servicing. That loss of revenue translates into a need for fewer mechanics and customer service representatives. One possible solution is for the government to require a higher percentage of electric automobile manufacturing to be produced in this country. Proponents of electric cars point to the jobs that will be created by the need to construct and maintain charging stations, new jobs manufacturing batteries, as well as cottage industries that will spring up to add specialized accessories for these vehicles.

## Jobs Lost to Green Technology

It is realistic to expect a significant percentage of people who currently are employed in the fossil fuel industry to lose their jobs. The question is how easy would it be to retrain these workers for green industries. Because such a high percentage of green jobs require a certificate rather than a college degree, educators are now considering adding such certificate programs to community colleges in areas where coal mining is declining.[12]

One problem is that because many of these workers are likely middle-aged or older, a significant number of them probably would not opt for retraining. A second issue is that production of coal energy requires almost twice as many more workers than those employed by natural gas and solar plants, while wind farms require even fewer workers. Studies do show that while some coal mining areas might also be ideal locations for wind power, wind energy's requirement for fewer workers will not make up the difference.[13] Still, a wind energy company in Wyoming has offered free training to displaced coal and natural gas workers.[14]

The problem with the decline of the fossil fuel industry is that much of it is concentrated in only a few states. That means these states' representatives in Congress have displayed their political clout by trying to keep fossil fuel production alive. One solution is for the government to subsidize displaced fossil fuel workers. Congress has approved funds to hire workers in coal mining states to clean up mines that have been closed. That will provide some temporary employment for displaced workers. New programs that represent a partnership of community colleges and green energy companies might prove attractive to some displaced workers, but what about the rest? As some experts predict coal will be phased out by 2030, one proposed solution for these workers is to offer them direct financial assistance and pay for it with a small tax on stock transactions.[15]

## Limitations to Growth

Much like cryptocurrency, the kinds of government regulations approved will determine whether it encourages or discourages green energy growth. The fossil fuel industry has its political clout and will resist reductions of its subsidies as well as approval of more subsidies for green energy. These subsidies are crucial though for these emerging technologies until they achieve enough volume to become cost-effective. Electric automobile growth will be predicated on regulations such as those in California that set deadlines for when new gas-powered automobile no longer would be sold. Given the substantial gas-powered automobile food chain, government help likely will be required to aid displaced workers such as those currently selling or manufacturing parts. So, while green technology is rapidly improving in the green energy and electric automobile fields, it will be government through its actions that determines how rapidly these technologies will be adopted and what provisions will be made for displaced workers.

## Likely Timetable for Growth

Economists forecast that by 2030, green economy will generate 24 million new jobs.[16] Figure 6.1 displays some future jobs likely to be created by green technology.

While that forecasted number of jobs might be a bit overly optimistic, I believe that the creation of between 15 million and 24 million new jobs is possible. The key to total net job growth will be determined by how effective governmental, educational, and corporate programs and

- Charging station installer
- Wind turbine technician
- Solar panel installer
- Green accounting specialist
- Water purification specialist
- Biofuel specialist
- Environmental lawyer
- Program manager, nonprofit environmental organization
- Environmental lawyer
- Carbon credits trader

*Figure 6.1 Some future green technology jobs*

partnerships are in transitioning those displaced workers willing to be retrained as well as easing the financial hardships of those displaced workers unwilling or unable to transition to new jobs in the green economy.

## Careers in Green Technology

Careers in green energy and sustainability are likely to be in demand for the foreseeable future. There are so many industries that offer green energy-related jobs. The current industry leaders in green-related jobs from most to least are construction, professional services, manufacturing, wholesale trade, other services, utilities, and agriculture.[17] A valuable website lists over 150 different careers in green energy and sustainability.[18] No matter what a person's interests, there is likely to be a matching green career.

## Majors and Centers of Instruction

Because green careers are so varied, it is not surprising that there are so many different majors that provide good preparation. Popular majors include environmental science, engineering, biology, zoology, chemistry, business management, and even, where it is offered, sustainability. Universities known for their undergraduate programs that prepare students for green careers include MIT, Harvard, Stanford, California Institute of Technology, Arizona State, University of Texas, University of Washington, and Cornell.[19]

## Short-Term Learning Opportunities

In addition to over 100 free online courses from Coursera and edX, there are a number of courses available online, often by university extension programs. Northern Arizona University, as an example, has a series of courses and certificate program in wind energy. Penn State's World Campus offers a graduate certificate in solar energy. It is expensive (over $9,000), but the 12 units apply toward a Master's degree in Renewable Energy and Sustainability Systems.

## Validating Knowledge for Those Already in Careers

Green energy and sustainability fields offer many ways for people already working to move into these areas. This excellent article includes several chapters on specific programs for people to *reskill* themselves to move into green fields.[20] Construction is clearly a green growth area. Someone already in this industry who wants to add green credentials might want to look at California State University at Chico's intriguing online program that includes courses and a voucher to take the LEED test to become a LEED Associate. The National Registry of Environmental Professionals offers various certifications (www.nrep.org) as does the National Board of Certified Energy Professionals (www.nabcep.org). For those people wanting to transfer their skills to a green career without starting over with an entry-level job should take a look at the book I coauthored on this topic.[21]

# CHAPTER 7

# The Internet of Things

When MIT researcher Kevin Ashton coined the phrase *The Internet of Things* (IoT) in 1999, it is unlikely he realized just how prevalent that technology would be today or why it is likely to grow astronomically in the future. The term refers to sensors attached to various objects that transmit their information via the Internet and, in turn, receive input and instructions back. The sensors can utilize a local area network or a 5G network to send information to a place where it can be stored in cloud servers and analyzed via data analytics. Often the term *smart* is used in conjunction with items that are part of the IoT. My home has a *smart* thermostat that enables me to monitor it and adjust my home's temperature wherever I happen to be. I own an Oura, a smart ring that can tell me how well I slept last night as well as how much exercise I'm getting.

Annoyingly, my iWatch will also *suggest* I stretch my legs when I've been sitting for an extended time. Smart watches monitor health and respond accordingly with recommendations. An automobile hit a friend of mine while he was crossing in a crosswalk. His watch sent a message to his wife and grown kids that he had suffered a fall. Today, there are the many *smart* devices in the home connected to an Amazon or Google device. These virtual assistants can respond to requests to turn on or off lights, order items, and so on. Remember the meter reader who used to come periodically to check electrical usage? Now a sensor sends that information back to the energy company.

## What Is Driving IoT Today?

Computer processing power continues to grow, while storage continues to decline in cost. At the same time, the cost of manufacturing sensors continues to drop. Wireless LANs are widespread, and the expansion of 5G networks combined with the sophistication today of data analytics are all factors driving the adoption of IoTs. Additionally, many companies are discovering that adding an IoT can increase the value of their products to their customers and bring them added revenue as well as more valuable information about their customers. Trucking companies can keep track of their trucks' locations and monitor how often their drivers stop for breaks. One IoT company offers smart tags for children to wear. For an additional fee, the tag can notify a parent if their child veers off the route to school.[1]

## IoT's Impact on the Health Care Industry

By 2025, forecasters predict, the IoT industry will hit between $1 trillion and $3 trillion in revenue due to a shift from providing mere connectivity to providing IoT-powered applications, platforms, and services. Health care is an area of rapid IoT growth in part because of the enormous growth of mobile devices, including smart watches, smart rings, smart phones, and so on. The *Internet of Medical Things* is forecast to grow to a $158 billion dollar market in 2022.[2] Patients now wear heart monitors to sense and record abnormal activity. Doctors can monitor patients' vital signs remotely and send *orders* to the sensors if additional information is needed or if a patient's condition worsens. The point is that the sensors provide real-time information. A new San Diego-based company has created an IoT device for monitoring opioid patients during their recovery.* Patients now can monitor their glucose levels with data that sensors send to their smartphones. The presence of 5G networks enable sensors to send blood pressure data as well as blood oxygen and heart rate levels to medical facilities where they can be reviewed in real time.

What about job losses or gains? At this point, whatever jobs might be lost by people who used to be required to administer test procedures to patients will be more than made up by the number of people who will

---

* "Institute-based Startup Receives Funding to Continue Development of Opioid Sensor." August 6, 2020. *UC San Diego Center News.* https://ucsdnews .ucsd.edu/pressrelease/qualcomm-institute-based-startup-receives-funding-to-continue-development-of-opioid-sensor (accessed April 28, 2022).

need to be hired to integrate and maintain IoT networks with existing health care IT equipment and, equally important, ensure cybersecurity.

## IoT's Impact on Transportation and Logistics

IoT networks in the transportation and logistics industry are projected to grow to a $40 billion market in 2022.[3] IoT transportation applications are not limited to the commercial sector. Superpedestrian is a company that sells a wheel that senses a riders' motions and boosts their pedaling power.[4] Smart cars require enormous numbers of sensors to feed information to controllers. These sensors keep track of everything, from the inflation level of tires to any danger in blind spots that the side cameras identify. For the self-driving mode, sensors have even more information to track. A car's navigation system also relies on sensors, as does the artificial intelligence required to interpret a driver's voice commands.

Commercial trucking companies use IoT networks to track their trucks and the performance of drivers, including a truck's fuel consumption to identify bad driving habits. IoT sensors also can provide the logistics required to track individual containers being transported. These sensors can track the temperature and condition of a specific container. An IoT network combined with blockchain technology can provide an accurate ledger of where specific items are at any given time for their entire journey from shipment to delivery. Added intelligence permits sensors to react to specific situations such as identification and notification if there are any specific alterations to a shipment's route and delivery time. While this use of IoT networks does not seem to cost people jobs, it does require additional personnel to train users and maintain the system as well as provide security.

## IoT's Impact in the Agriculture Industry

The agricultural industry, particularly large companies, has embraced the use of IoT networks. Nokia has been promoting what it calls *smart agriculture*, which it identifies as IoT networks that can, for example, automate a greenhouse so that it maintains the right amount of humidity and its plants receive just the right amount of water. Sensors placed in fields can monitor soil moisture and acidity.⁵ An IoT also can monitor sensors on drones to identify pests and count fruits. Although some tractor manufacturers have been experimenting with self-driving tractors, there are still a number of problems with that concept, including lack of sufficient battery life. The sales proposition is not that these tractors would eliminate some employees, but that it would *free up* a farmer to perform other tasks. Agriculture is an example of an industry that employs the least educated group of workers. The tightening of the border has made it more difficult for this industry to find people to perform tasks such as picking fruits and vegetables. The technology has not progressed to the point where certain fruits can be picked by machines in a cost-effective way. If technology improves significantly, this might be an area where IoT impacts jobs.

## IoT's Impact in the Energy Sector

*Smart cities* refer to cities that have widely deployed IoT technology. Sensors in the roads can track traffic and adjust lights accordingly. Streetlights can adjust to the amount of light present, and cities can monitor their water supplies and usage of energy. As I mentioned earlier, it used to be a common sight to see meter readers walking through neighborhoods to read electricity and gas meters. Today, IoT technology has eliminated those positions. The government has directed appliance manufacturers to produce STAR ratings for an appliance's energy efficiency. Appliances are not just becoming more energy efficient, but IoT technology is making them a lot smarter. Samsung now manufactures a smart refrigerator that is advertised as capable of serving as a hub of a smart kitchen. Its panel allows customers to shop for groceries, find recipes on the Internet, or use cameras inside the refrigerator to see which items need reordering. In the future, such smart appliances will have even greater functionality. Amazon has filed a patent for a smart refrigerator that would be capable of sensing which food has spoiled.⁶

## IoT's Impact in the Retail Industry

The retail industry has embraced IoT technology. Sensors can track inventory on shelves and locate items that have been misplaced. Loss prevention tags enable retailers to cut theft, but they also make it possible for customers to pick up items and then self-checkout without the need for a cashier. I was astounded a few years ago to discover that retailers were tracking the performance of their end cap displays, generally the most expensive real estate in a store, by using sensors and cameras to track when a customer picked up an item from an end cap and then tracking the item to see if the customer actually paid for it or returned it to the end cap. Sophisticated cameras actually gauged customers' interest in items by measuring the dilation of their eyes. Retailers now our using Bluetooth Low Energy (BLE) beacons to track customers' movements in retail stores and offer them targeted sale items. I wrote a science fiction story a few years ago on that topic, but now science fiction has become reality.

## Current Limitations of IoT Technology

The IoT has made major strides in the past few years, but obstacles remain. Two major problems are security and platform interoperability. Already companies have found their internal IT structures attacked via the hacking of their IoT network. The rush to get new IoT products out the door and increase revenue has taken preference over ensuring that the products have adequate security in some cases. Because this market is growing so quickly, manufacturers have not focused on interoperability among different platforms. This lack of interoperability impacts larger companies with complex IT infrastructures that span several different computing platforms. A third issue is the fact that 5G networks are not yet widely available. Their speed will greatly enhance the performance and value of IOT networks.

## The IoT's Impact on Jobs

The general consensus on IoT technology's impact on jobs is that it will result in a net increase of jobs, but it will cost many workers with the least education their positions as sensors replace the need for manual labor. There will be an astronomical increase in the number of IT professionals needed to design, build, and manage IoT networks. In fact, the entire IoT food chain will benefit because of increased demand for developers,

- IOT traffic specialist
- IOT cybersecurity specialist
- IOT programmer
- IOT agricultural specialist
- IOT sensor installer
- IOT repair specialist
- IOT medical device developer
- IOT home specialist
- Smart car programmer
- Smart greenhouse specialist

*Figure 7.1 Some future IoT jobs*

manufacturers, resellers, and retailers. McKinsey examined the IoT market and concluded that around 30 percent of it was focused on hardware, while the remaining 70 percent was split between software and services. Its analysts predicted that jobs would be distributed according to this split. Many companies likely will outsource the security of their IoT networks to services that specialize in that area. People with cybersecurity skills and some knowledge of IoT technology will be in great demand.[7] Figure 7.1 lists some future IoT jobs.

## Timetable for Widespread Adoption

Even the most conservative forecasts for IoT growth are astounding, but they do pass the *sniff test* because no one can argue with the exploding number of wearable devices and mobile phones or the cost-effectiveness of IoT networks. There is one statistic, though, that I found astounding, and it is one that will hinder IoT's growth. It appears that 84 percent of companies that have deployed IoT technology have experienced a security breach.[8] That's an incredible number! Still, even if I reduce the more conservative growth estimates for this industry by 50 percent, I'm left with a still very impressive 10 percent annual growth rate for the next couple of years. I believe that the industry will address security concerns, and by 2025, growth will accelerate to more than 20 percent. Ironically, job growth will increase far more than the industry's growth rate because there is such a need for security personnel. I should add that one of the other emerging technologies I discuss in the next chapter would also spur IoT technology growth. Virtual and augmented reality relies on sensors so people can touch and feel virtual objects. As this market grows, there will be more need for IoT networks.

# IoT Careers

The IoT is a great career opportunity, particularly for anyone interested in technology. The hottest areas right now are in IoT architecture and design, embedded systems, networking, and security. There are also opportunities for people more interested in a business focus within the IoT industry or a management position in a company that currently has an IoT network or plans on implementing one. What is very appealing at this time is that, although the technology is not new, there is only one undergraduate degree program that I have found, although there are a number of schools that offer graduate education in this field. What that means is that there are far fewer *gatekeepers* to keep people from entering the field because they don't have a particular degree.

# Majors and Centers of Instruction

Florida International University offers a Bachelor's of Science degree in the IoT. A number of universities offer graduate programs led by Stanford's School of Engineering. Others include Northeastern University, the University of New Mexico, the University of Buffalo, UC Berkeley, Florida International University, and the University of Illinois. This list is growing all the time. Virtually, all of these programs are offered through engineering departments.

# Short-Term Learning Opportunities

There are a number of excellent online courses as well as online certification programs. Programs from edX (edx.org) and Coursera (Coursera .org) provide excellent introductions to the field. Stanford's School of Engineering offers a free course, and Cisco offers a free 20-hour program. In fact, in 2022, over 300 free courses are available online.[†] For more business-oriented people who want to have a general understanding of IoT, the Cloud Credential Council offers such a certificate program

---

[†] "300+ Internet of Things Courses 2022 Learn Online for Free." n.d. classcentral .com. www.classcentral.com/subject/internet-of-things.

(cloudcredential.org). The University of California's Irvine campus' extension division offers a certificate program in the IoT.

## Validating Knowledge for Those Already in Careers

By far, the easiest way for people to validate their knowledge of the IoT field without earning a formal degree is to earn a certificate. Equally important, it is now possible to validate knowledge of IoT through a testing process. CertNexus (certnexus.com) offers a test for IoT practitioners as well as a separate test for IoT security practitioners.

# CHAPTER 8

# Virtual Reality

Virtual reality (VR) is a technology that totally immerses someone in a simulated reality. Augmented reality is a technology that augments reality. In other words, people might wear special glasses that enable them to view a restaurant and then see an overlay of customer reviews for it. Mixed reality is where the real world is *augmented* in such a way that people see the real world but can also perform virtual tasks within that world. An example of this technology is furniture fitting where a piece of virtual furniture can be placed in a real environment. As VR is the more general term for simulated environments, we'll use that term the rest of this chapter to describe simulated reality of any kind.

## The Metaverse

The metaverse refers to an immersive digital simulated world that is now in its infancy. People's digital representatives or avatars in the near future will roam through this digital world and encounter a world of digital storefronts, concerts, other avatars, educational institutions, and so on. It would serve as the natural evolution of the mobile Internet but with an immersive quality. Already companies are training new employees by having them don VR headsets to *travel* to different parts of their operations in ways far more likely to hold their interests than merely listening to a lecture. The metaverse will create all kinds of job opportunities, including digital commerce as avatars order real food for delivery from a metaverse storefront. There will be a need for digital designers, content creators, and trainers. On the other hand, the creation of AI bots that perform customer service tasks in this digital world will eliminate low-level jobs.[1] The metaverse is steaming full-speed ahead. The Metaverse Standards Forum now exists with Microsoft, Meta, Epic, Unity, and over 1,000 other companies. In fact, according to Matthew Ball, a Silicon Valley insider and the author of *The Metaverse*, seven of the 11 largest companies in the world have committed their "their businesses, their organizational models, their capital spending and their product lines to this."[2]

How many jobs will the metaverse produce, or will it even produce jobs? One critic believes that it will perpetuate the current situation where digital elites (software and hardware engineers and others with world building capabilities) will flourish, while others will be regulated to the gig economy.[3] Meta hired a consulting firm to conduct an independent study of the potential job growth of the metaverse. Its conclusion of an enormous economic impact on global economies was based on an assumption that the growth of the metaverse will parallel and even exceed the growth of the mobile Internet.[4] That assumption is debatable. Interestingly enough, McKinsey analysts interviewed over 3,000 corporate respondents and concluded that companies already are investing substantial amounts of cash in the metaverse in hopes of not being left behind. The leading industries investing the highest percentage of their digital budgets on the metaverse over the next three to five years are: energy (18 percent), automotive, machinery and assembly (17 percent), high tech (17 percent), tourism (15 percent), and media/entertainment (15 percent).[5]

## The Current State of VR Technology

VR has been around since Sega first unveiled a product at the 1993 Consumer Electronics trade show. The company wound up canceling that product before its release. For many years, VR was bulky, expensive, and primitive because of the limited state of technology. Despite that, investors have kept pouring money into VR companies. One writer in a very snarky overview of the VR market described it as the "white rich kid of technology."[6]

Better graphics and headsets today as well as more sophisticated software have VR manufacturers optimistic about the future. While the major sales at this time have been in the gaming area, other industries are starting to show growth. In some ways, the market reminds me of the early personal computer market. When I managed one of the first computer stores, my customers asked me what practical things they could do with that technology. Eventually, the hardware and software improved, and applications appeared that made multiple PCs per household the norm.

# The Current VR Job Market

Flush with investor capital, VR companies are in hiring mode, although the industry currently only employees around a half million people directly or indirectly.[7] There is great demand for software and hardware engineers, trainers, and anyone with computer graphics or world-building skills.

# VR in Education

One area where VR technology is a natural fit is in education. Arizona State University has created an immersive world in which students can learn biology. In fact, Goldman Sachs forecasts that the education sector will have 25 million VR users by 2025.[8] Whether students interact with the signers of the Declaration of Independence, take a trip inside a human body, or travel to ancient Rome or Greece, the potential educational uses of VR technology are countless.

# VR in Health Care

One of the earliest uses of VR technology in the health care field was having surgeons practice surgeries via a VR application. Medical students can now perform dissection virtually as well as *examine* patients. Patients suffering from pain can be distracted via VR, while patients suffering from agoraphobia can use VR to adjust to that condition.[9]

# VR in Gaming

The VR gaming market in 2020 produced around $15 billion dollars in revenue, and revenue is projected to reach $92 billion by 2027, with a cumulative annual growth rate of 30 percent during the period 2020 through 2027.*

Experts cite the COVID-19 pandemic that kept many people at home as one reason for the dramatic increase in VR gaming, and they also add, the uniqueness of 360-degree views, the lure of real-time interaction

---

* See www.grandviewresearch.com/industry-analysis/virtual-reality-in-gaming-market.

with other players, and the more sophisticated gloves and headsets as additional drivers.

## VR in Entertainment

While gaming has taken the lead in VR-related revenue, entertainment is likely to rival it in the future. VR is likely to be deployed in movie theaters, concerts, and sports venues so that attendees can enjoy enhanced experiences. A moviegoer could become a part of the Marvel universe, while NBA game attendees could have their experiences augmented by viewing key analytics in real time. VR is already becoming a part of concerts as Justin Bieber and Ariana Grande have performed life shows within the metaverse. Katy Perry believes in the next decade, people will attend concerts via the metaverse.[10]

## VR in Training

Training is a natural market for VR technology, although cost is definitely still a factor in adoption. A PricewaterhouseCoopers' study found that VR training becomes cost-effective when there are more than 3,000 students involved.[11] One interesting new VR application by Tailspin enables people to practice firing someone. The virtual figure sobs and complains just as a real person would to the news.[12]

VR is ideal for simulating extraordinary environments. NASA recently advertised for volunteers willing to spend a year in a special 1,700 square foot facility in Houston that simulates life on Mars.[13]

## VR in Museums

Museums are a good fit for VR technology. Not only can patrons experience an immersive experience, but with the use of augmented reality, they also can view items and then see additional information. A number of museums are now experimenting with this technology. I'm differentiating this onsite use of VR in museums from the efforts many museums have made to create *virtual* online tours via websites. This type of interaction became very popular during a time when the pandemic closed many museums.

## VR in Manufacturing

Manufacturers are bullish on the uses of VR technology. A panel of manufacturers cited several examples of VR use in their industry, including assembly, end-of-line inspections, changeovers, and training.[14]

## VR in Marketing

Meta has been beating the drums for the advantages of a metaverse. Companies such as Pepsi and Mercedes Benz have begun using VR technology in their marketing. Lowes created a VR environment for customers to visualize how its products would fit into their homes, while McDonalds has included a VR headset based on Google's Cardboard product inside its Happy Meals.[†] While there are numerous other examples, the real explosive growth is coming as marketers stake out their property claims on the metaverse. Imagine, for example, virtual storefronts that sell everything imaginable and allow participants to handle the merchandise and the make a purchase. The actual product would ship immediately. One major advantage to small company marketers is that they do not have to lease brick-and-mortar stores or develop elaborate websites. If they hire a VR services company, they can appear to be a much larger company and compete on a more equal footing with far larger competitors.

## Current Limitations of the Technology

While VR technology has made major strides in recent years, there are still limitations. The headsets are still too heavy and bulky. Some users experience locomotion sickness, and there is some concern by the medical community that excessive use of VR equipment could lead to addiction. There also is some concern over the danger of eye damage.[15]

---

[†] "Examples of Successful Virtual Reality Marketing." January 19, 2018. digitalmarketinginstitute.com. https://digitalmarketinginstitute.com/blog/7-examples-of-successful-virtual-reality-marketing (accessed April 28, 2022).

## Likely Timetable for Widespread Adoption

Despite the current limitations, most experts expect the VR industry to finally take off, and the period from now through 2030 should experience explosive growth with 23 million jobs related to VR or AR by 2030. One encouraging sign is that a study revealed that 19 percent of consumers have tried VR technology.[16] Figure 8.1 lists some future VR Jobs.

## VR Careers

This field is gaining momentum fueled by investor-funded startups as well as established companies such as Meta (formally Facebook) and Google. Technical career paths include content developer, designers, software engineers, gaming engineers, and user experience designer. For people with some knowledge of VR but with a business focus, there are careers in business development, program management, community managers, finance, and so on.

## Majors and Centers of Instruction

Very few universities offer a formal undergraduate degree in VR. In 2018, Drexel University became the first university to offer a *Bachelor* of Science degree in *Virtual Reality* and Immersive Media (VRIM). Ringling College of Art and Design offers the first VR Development degree, a BFA in Virtual Reality Development. This list is growing all the time. San Jose State, Georgia Institute of Technology, and Old Dominion have added programs. As gaming is now such a major part of the VR market, it is possible to gain entry by learning to code and design games. The University of Southern California ranks as the top school in games and design and offers an undergraduate degree in that subject.

- VR curriculum specialist
- VR marketing specialist
- VR real estate specialist
- VR advertising specialist
- VR application developer
- VR game developer
- VR graphic designer
- VR story specialist
- VR hardware designer
- VR therapist

*Figure 8.1 Some future VR jobs*

Depending on what aspect of VR is of most interest, students at most universities will major in software engineering or computer science. Many of the leading universities for graduate education in VR areas such as MIT and Stanford permit undergraduate computer science students to take elective courses in VR topics.

## Short-Term VR Learning Opportunities

This is one field where the ability to code is far more important than a degree. There is a wealth of online courses as well as certificate programs. Coursera, Udemy, and edX offer courses and certificate programs. Unity offers its own certificate program for Unity VR Developers. The Global Technical Council (Globaltechcouncil.org) offers several professional certificate programs.

Several community colleges offer certificate programs. Cochise College, for example, offers a certificate for a VR technologist, while Mount San Antonio College offers a certificate for a VR designer. Universities also offer certificate programs through their extension departments. MIT offers a certificate program through its Sloan Executive Management department while the University of California's San Diego campus offers a self-paced online certificate for VR application development. NYU's Tandon School of Engineering offers a certificate in AR/VR development and 3D graphics.

## Validating Knowledge for Those Already in Careers

The career path for people already in the workforce starts with validating their knowledge of this technology through one or more online certificate programs. For technically oriented people, the transition is relatively easy. Software engineers need to add a VR development-specific certificate and start building a portfolio of VR applications that demonstrate their hands-on ability. GitHub.com is an ideal place to upload this code. They then should plan on attending some of the VR trade shows to meet with companies and make connections. Another excellent way to connect with industry insiders is to join a local VR meetup group (meetup.com).

# CHAPTER 9

# Big Data

Big Data refers to massive datasets. One method of characterizing their components is by referring to the *five Vs*: volume, velocity, variety, veracity, and value. That means that these datasets are unique because of their sheer size, the speed by which they are increasing, the fact the data contains a variety of different types, the quality of the data, and its value.

## Big Data Is Only Going to Grow

Data are accumulating at an astounding pace. Consider all the social media generated each day, add the data from billions of sensors in IoT networks, add to that number medical records including X-rays, insurance paperwork, test results, and so on, and don't forget all the records companies keep on customer interactions. International Data Corporation (IDC) forecasts the amount of data in the world will grow from 33 zettabytes in 2018 to 175 zettabytes in 2025.[1] If you're not familiar with a zettabyte, you're not alone. A zettabyte represents one billion terabytes. Social media and online businesses generate an astounding amount of data. Google, Facebook, Microsoft, and Amazon store at least 1,200 petabytes of information.[2] A petabyte is equivalent to a million gigabytes.

## Drivers of Big Data

Several elements have converged to drive momentum for Big Data as an industry. Data storage has become less expensive, and new storage architecture has developed to handle enormous datasets. In addition, analytical tools, including artificial intelligence, have become far more sophisticated and readily available. Around 20 percent of data are structured in a form that traditional database software can handle. An example would be a list of addresses. Unstructured data consist of all kinds of different forms, including photos, social media, graphics, X-rays, and so on. Artificial intelligence has come to the rescue and now offers a way to analyze unstructured data.[3]

Another driver is Moore's law. Computer processing power has grown continually and is now capable of processing large datasets. Finally, the data themself continue to increase each year. Equally important to all the technological advances driving Big Data is the realization by corporations that their data are a valuable commodity.

## The Use of Artificial Intelligence for Analytics

The analytics artificial intelligence provides can take many different forms. It can be descriptive and simply show results. It can be diagnostic and determine what causes a certain business program. It can be predictive and determine certain trends likely to occur in the future. Finally, it can be prescriptive and provide actionable information on what a company needs to do to take preemptive action. One example of this approach is a manufacturing company that uses analytics to determine which machines need preemptive maintenance to eliminate problems before the machine fails.*

## Big Data and Personal Information

Back in 2016, a reporter pointed out that companies had an average of 75,000 different data points on individuals.[4] Remember that was a time well before social media really took off. Imagine how many data points someone in his teens will generate just from Snapchat, Instagram, Twitter, Facebook, and so on before reaching middle age. Another factor is how so many companies are starting to utilize IoT data from the billions of sensors already in operation. These sensors provide real-time information that can provide vital information much like the metaphor of a canary in a coalmine. You may have read that water pressure dropped noticeably

---

* "What Is Big Data Analytics and Why Is It So Important?" April 3, 2022. simplilearn.com. www.simplilearn.com/what-is-big-data-analytics-article (accessed May 4, 2022).

when very highly viewed television shows had commercials, whether that meant the old Milton Berle show, *I love Lucy*, or one of the Super Bowl broadcasts. When my son was in the Peace Corps in Romania in the early 1990s, the government did not have enough hot water capacity for its population. One way it controlled the flow in Bucharest was by scheduling hot water availability for the hour when the single most popular TV show was broadcast. Believe it or not, that show was the American soap opera Dallas. Today, prescriptive analytics could be used to make such recommendations. Amazon, Spotify, Netflix, and other corporations use their customer data to make recommendations for content likely to please them, whether those recommendations take the form of book titles, movie titles, songs, or something else.

One of the stages of preparing Big Data is the veracity or accuracy of that data. I have a Facebook account and my wife doesn't. Almost every day she uses my sign-in information (with my encouragement) to see what our friends are doing. She often will *like* pictures of babies, something I never do. She also will browse ads that are meant to appeal to women her age. I smile whenever I think of the distorted analytics Mark Zukerberg's company has determined from my profile and is selling to its customers.

## Big Data in the Financial and Insurance Sectors

Big Data's role is growing in financial institutions. Analysts can use analytical tools to detect correlations between specific events and the stock market's rise or fall. When someone hacked my system a year ago, my credit card company used analytics to detect buying patterns that did not match my profile. Another major use of analytics we are starting to see is in risk appraisal. Artificial intelligence tools can sift through mountains of personal data to determine just how likely it is for potential customers to pay their bills. Now, imagine how disruptive this technology could be to traditional banks if a startup uses such tools to give far quicker approval of loans than more traditional rivals. Similarly, these tools could be used to determine whether or not an insurance company should offer insurance to a potential client. Imagine for a moment the sheer volume of personal data available on an individual who seeks an insurance policy. That person's driving record, marital status, age, educational background, religion, product purchase history (including cigarettes), and so on, all could lead to an informed yes or no decision. Equally important for a startup seeking to disrupt an industry, it could use analytics to make that decision far faster than a more insurance company relying on humans rather than automation. Without the need to pay humans, that startup probably could price its insurance far lower and gain a competitive advantage.

## Big Data in Marketing

From a marketing perspective, customer data are the most valuable corporate asset. Based on previous purchases, Amazon's Alexa now offers unsolicited advice on additional products a customer might want to purchase. The advantage of analytics is that artificial intelligence can discern patterns in customer buying habits that are not apparent even to the most sophisticated marketing professional. There is an often-repeated anecdote that a major retailer started sending advertisements for pregnancy-related products to a teenage girl. Her father protested that the material was irrelevant and inappropriate, and it turns out the company had inferred that the teen was pregnant because she purchased certain moisturizer products that the data showed other pregnant women purchased. The father apparently then discovered that his daughter really was pregnant.

Pricing decisions is one marketing area where Big Data excels. Analytics can recommend that a hotel raise its prices a certain week because a major entertainment event is scheduled nearby and the best dynamic pricing for McDonalds on an hourly or day of the week.[5]

Another key marketing area where analytics is invaluable is in customer profiling and predicting what products such customers might want in the future. I once served as a research director for a business-to-business market research company that collected technology-related information on hundreds of thousands of companies. One day, I met with an executive who apologized and said he had double-booked the time he was supposed to spend with me. I told him that I had planned on profiling his customers and explaining how he could find thousands of additional potential customers most likely to meet that profile. Keep in mind that companies that sell their products through distributors really don't know much about their customers. He canceled his other meeting and wound up buying the data from my company. Indeed's jobseekers' website describes how moisturizer marketers match data on their own customers with social media data on people to determine the social media users most likely to become their customers.[6]

Big Data can help with the four *Ps* of marketing. *Promotion* is an area where analytics can help marketers make informed decisions on where to spend their advertising budget. Big Data can provide insight on what periodicals their customers read, what television shows they watch, where they spend their time online, and so on. As far as *Place* goes, Big Data can determine where customers prefer to buy their products. Do they buy online primarily, or do they prefer going to their local retailer? Big Data can help with the actual *Product* as well by predicting what specific functionality, branding, and services customers want.

## Big Data's Use in Human Resources

Human resources (HR) is an area where Big Data are proving invaluable. HR departments use this set of analytical tools and data to analyze job applicants and predict who is the best fit for the company. In addition, HR departments can use existing employee data to analyze those characteristics found in the best performing employees and then use those criteria to match people in the candidate pool. In the near future, HR departments will broaden their use of Big Data to include the massive amount of social media data. Someone who tweeted years ago about the evils of a *greedy* corporation might wonder in the future if that were the reason that company rejected him for a job. Does Instagram contain pictures you posted of yourself at wild parties while you were in college? That data might not age well when they become part of the Big Data lake a company accesses when considering you for a job in the future.

## Big Data's Use in the Health Care Industry

The health care industry is starting to utilize Big Data and analytics to manage and leverage the massive amount of diverse patient information it has. The analytics might turn out to be predictive and help determine which patients are likely to require certain medications and treatments in the near future, or it could be diagnostic and reveal a serious problem that wasn't even on the radar of a health care facility. It might be prescriptive and recommend staffing changes to optimize intake and outtake patterns or descriptive and provide a visual display of revenue patterns. Blue Cross/Blue Shield worked with an analytics firm to go through insurance and pharmacy data to identify 742 risk factors for predicting whether someone is at risk for abusing opioids.[7]

## Current Obstacles to Big Data's Rapid Growth

There are a number of current obstacles that limit rapid growth of Big Data. One problem is that corporations often have data silos where data are hoarded and protected jealously by department managers rather than being integrated corporatewide. A second major hurdle is the continuing threat security breaches pose. The third obstacle is just as critical; there is an enormous shortage of trained data engineers and scientists. As far back as 2012, McKinsey's analysts forecast a shortage of 140,000 to 190,000 data personnel with deep analytical skills and 1.5 million managers who had the knowledge necessary to make decisions based on the information the analytics provided.[†]

## Prospects for Future Growth

One new trend has been the growth of services companies that provide expertise and solve the problem many companies have in finding qualified employees for in-house management and analysis of its Big Data. Many universities and training organizations are starting to offer online courses and certificates in Big Data areas, while *bootcamps* are springing up to offer intensive short-term training to fill the gaps in trained personnel. Industry watchers forecast a 30 percent increase in jobs for data science professionals between 2022 and 2026. That would represent over 11 million new jobs![8]

---

[†] Quoted in M. McDonald. August 6, 2013. "How Big Data Will Impact Employment and Human Resources."

## Likely Timetable for Explosive Growth

Surveys show that over 90 percent of corporate executives polled are planning on increasing the amounts they spend on Big Data projects.[9] Assuming that cybersecurity concerns are resolved and the data scientist shortage ameliorates because of more people entering this field or because services companies expand to fill the gap, growth of Big Data should really take off by 2026.

## Future Jobs in Big Data

A number of new jobs will be created as Big Data really takes off. The profound ethical and privacy issues raised by so much information about individuals will create a need for data ethicists, both in government and in large companies. As the number of enormous datasets proliferates, opportunities will arise for brokers to serve as middlemen for information. Cybersecurity concerns will create the need for specialists focusing on securing the data. In addition, as quantum computing becomes a reality rather than just theoretical, a new specialization, engineers who can take quantum computing data and then manage to fold it into existing large datasets, will develop.[10] Figure 9.1 lists some of the future jobs in Big Data.

## Big Data Careers

Northeastern University is known for its very pragmatic approach to education because it prepares its students so well for the world of work. Its website described the opportunities in data science in glowing terms and pointed out that Glassdoor rated this field number one for four years in a row. It also pointed out that the U.S. Bureau of Labor Forecasts 27.9 percent growth in this area through 2026.[11] It is almost impossible

- Big Data scientist
- Big Data researcher
- Big Data corporate manager
- Big Data analytics specialist
- Big Data cybersecurity specialist
- Big Data consultant
- Big Data ethicist

*Figure 9.1 Some future Big Data jobs*

to overestimate the career opportunities in data science, including Big Data and analytics.

## Majors and Centers of Instruction

There are several universities that now offer undergraduate degrees in data analytics and/or data science,‡ but it is not necessary to major specifically in that field. The most common majors for students interested in a career in data science include computer science, software engineering, information technology, and applied mathematics and statistics. Obviously, the emphasis is on plenty of mathematics and computer programming, as well as exposure to databases. Many senior positions in this field require advanced degrees.

## Short-Term Learning Opportunities

There are several worthwhile online certificate programs. The University of California's San Diego campus offers a six-course certificate program in Big Data through Coursera, and Google also offers a certificate program in data analytics through Coursera. Eureka and Udemy also offer certificate programs. It is possible that a local community college might also offer a certificate in this field.

## Validating Knowledge for Those Already in Careers

Career changers should find data science a very intriguing opportunity given the severe shortages in qualified people and the robust growth rate it is likely to experience. While certificate programs are one way to validate knowledge, a more intensive approach for those already working is a bootcamp that focuses on Big Data and analytics. *CIO Magazine* recently published a list of the top 15 bootcamps.[12]

Another way to break into this field is to attend one of the major Big Data trade shows. Often, there are tutorials as well as ample opportunities to meet with people area in this field. Just put *Big Data trade shows* in a search engine and you'll be surprised just how many different events there are.

---

‡ www.mastersindatascience.org/specialties/bachelor-degrees-in-data-science/.

# CHAPTER 10

# Genomics and Human Augmentation

## Genomics and Gene Editing With CRISPR

For many years, scientists have been trying to map the DNA and genetic structure of humanity, known as the human genome. Finally, in 2022, they completed this project and identified over 100 new genes as well as millions of gene variations.[1] Genomics is the multidisciplinary field that focuses on genomes for various organisms, including humans, as well on techniques for manipulating these genes. Jennifer Doudna and Emmanuelle Charpentier received the 2020 Nobel Prize in Chemistry for their work in discovering Clustered Regularly Interspaced Short Palindromic Repeats (CRISPR), a very efficient method of editing genes.

## Why Is CRISPR So Important?

Scientists have used other methods for gene editing, but they were very time consuming and not as effective or efficient. CRISPR is based on a very clever way that bacteria manage to protect themselves from viruses. They produce enzymes to fight specific viruses and then store that information in their own genome as portraits of these same viruses. They then use this information to fight off those viruses' attacks in the future by creating *attack* enzymes composed of Cas9. Scientists discovered that they could fool Cas9 enzymes by feeding them an RNA sample that matches the DNA segment that needs editing. These enzymes then will find a match and cut up its DNA. Doudna and Charpentier refined this process so that scientists could snip a strand of DNA at a specific location to edit a gene.

One very practical example of why this new streamlined approach is so important is that, eventually, after extensive testing and government approval, it will make it possible in the case where a single gene is responsible for a disease to edit that defective gene and cure the patient. Sickle cell disease is an example of a very painful condition in Afro-Americans caused by a single gene. Genomics offers the promise of breakthroughs in a number of different industries and not just health care.

## Forces Driving Widespread Adoption of Genomics

There are several drivers creating momentum for the genomics industry. One is the enormous amount of money that pharmaceutical companies and investment firms have plowed into genomic startups. One recent article identified the top 30 startups in this field.[2] In fact, in 2020, MSCI's Genomic Index registered gains of over 40 percent while tracking around 250 different companies in this field. A second driver is the speed with which CRISPR enables scientists to edit genes. The speed with which drug companies using this technique were able to develop COVID-19 vaccines is ample proof of what a game changer this approach is for the pharmaceutical industry. Competition for patents in this potentially lucrative field is driving this investment feeding frenzy.

## Medical Applications of Genomics

Scientists point to a number of applications using CRISPR to treat diseases caused by a single defective gene. That's likely to be the first type of gene editing to be approved because it is far more certain what the outcome of such a procedure would be. Besides sickle cell disease, beta thalassemia, a blood-based disorder, also seems a likely candidate for treatment. Using CRISPR would be far more effective than the current therapy of regular blood transfusions, with the only other option being a bone marrow transplant.[3] The pharmaceutical industry is developing a number of very practical applications of CRISPR.

Scientists doing animal research on the impact of specific genes in order to develop drugs to treat certain ailments can use CRISPR to knock out a specific gene and then observe the impact on the animal whose genes have been edited. The speed advantage CRISPR offers in such experiments is critical to rapid development of such drugs. There is a lot of excitement in the pharmaceutical industry over the ways that CRISPR could facilitate the development of new cancer treatments.[4] It could enable scientists to screen cancer cells and quickly determine which genes are enabling those cells to reproduce rapidly. What could be breathtaking in the distant future is that drug companies could customize drugs for specific patients.

## Agricultural Applications of Genomics

Agriculture is a field where CRISPR already is starting to make an impact. One study found that genomics results in a 6× increase in income for some farmers.[5] Genomics can help scientists develop crops with higher yields, immunity to common diseases, and with the ability to thrive in environments with poor soil, low water, high temperatures, and high humidity. Given the already tangible effects of climate change, there is momentum for developing drought-tolerant crops. Other agricultural applications in the future include algae that produce oil that can be turned into biofuel and food that resists spoilage. Crops also could be modified to be insect resistant.

## Other Industries Impacted by Genomics

Gene editing has applications in other industries as well. A consultancy that tracks genomics sees opportunities for developing everything from new fragrances to cleaning products. Exxon in conjunction with a genomics startup created algae that produces twice as much fat that can be turned into oil that can be used as biofuel.*

## Current Limitations to Growth of Genomics

There are a number of obstacles that constrain growth of this industry. The lack of trained personnel is critical. A second problem is the cost of

---

* "Healthcare Is Only the Beginning: 15 Big Industries CRISPR Technology Could Disrupt." August 1, 2018. cbinsights.com. www.cbinsights.com/research/crispr-industries-disruption/ (accessed May 2, 2022).

clinical procedures and the question of whether insurance would even cover these in the future. Equally pressing issues today are concerns about future regulations. The industry would prefer to govern itself, but there is mounting pressure from various government agencies because of the public's concern about the possibilities of designer babies and the revival of eugenics-type human experimentation.

Despite the fact that leading figures and organizations in this field agreed to put the brakes on any human experimentation, a Chinese researcher decided to ignore these prohibitions and produced twin girls who were genetically modified. The Chinese government did imprison this researcher, but a precedent had been set. Any new confirmed reports of human experimentation using gene editing techniques will definitely push governments toward establishing the very restrictive regulations that industry leaders would like to avoid.

## Timetable for Explosive Growth of Genomics

Industry forecasters predict that the global genomics market will grow from $27.81 billion in 2021 to $94.65 billion in 2028.[6] Despite current obstacles, this forecast seems reasonable because of the volume of investments pouring in. The lack of adequate personnel will keep growth from accelerating even faster, but some companies have started to retrain existing employees. This use of *reskilling* is bound to grow as a trend. Another interesting trend is the use of simulations to train employees in the new techniques required for genomic research. Virtual reality technology has advanced to a level where such simulations have real educational value.

## Future Job Opportunities in Genomics

Job prospects are very bright in this industry, but it is likely to disrupt several current business practices. The cancer treatment industry is enormous. Imagine the impact a cancer breakthrough that cures rather than treats cancer and how it would affect jobs in that industry. Work on making pig organs more acceptable for human transplants by using gene splicing could impact organ transplants in a major way, while oil created from algae that can be converted to biofuel impacts the petroleum market but creates new jobs in the biofuel industry. New agricultural products created through genomics will require additional personnel in manufacturing, logistics, marketing, sales, and other areas. It is likely that the genomics field will create far more jobs than it displaces. Besides the technical jobs that require extensive science backgrounds, startups as well as more established companies will need to staff up their finance, marketing, sales, IT, and other departments as well.

## Human Augmentation

While attention recently has focused on genomics and the breakthroughs in gene editing, another trend in biotechnology has been growing. Cyborgs were once the province of science fiction, but now they are very real. The term *cyborg* is a combination of *cybernetics* and *organism*, in other words, a human whose abilities have been extended by appending some machine functionality. Known among themselves as *grinders* or *biohackers*, enthusiasts are driven by a number reasons, including overcoming physical handicaps, wanting to expand human capabilities, and desiring to increase their longevity.

### Overcoming Physical Handicaps

One of the earliest efforts at biohacking came from the necessity of overcoming physical handicaps. Whether it was someone trying to replace limbs, see or hear again, or regain lose strength, biohackers have made enormous progress. Adam Gorlitsky, a man paralyzed from the waist down, walked a marathon in a little under 34 hours using an assistive robotic exoskeleton.[7] A partially blind filmmaker created his own electronic eye using a camera. Others can view what he sees through that camera as well.[8]

Augmented hearing has been around for quite a while in the form of cochlear implants as well, of course, in the form of hearing aids. Finally, when it comes to losing muscular strength as we age, biohackers have solved that problem with the use of exoskeletons. One popular model in Japan where there is an aging population is an exoskeleton that enables wears to lift up to 55 pounds by using air pressure to pump up the mechanical muscles.[9]

### The Desire to Expand Human Capabilities

One of the early researchers in the field of biohacking is Professor Kevin Warwick of Reading University. He implanted an RFID sensor in his shoulder that he uses to switch on lights, open doors as he enters rooms, and even switch on lights as he enters a room.[10] Warwick's experiments include learning to control an electric wheelchair with an artificial hand and communicating with his wife via electrodes both had embedded in their arms.[†] Advanced research into links between the human brain and computers are underway today at Neuralink, the Alfred E. Mann Foundation, and several universities.

## Future Biotechnology and Human Augmentation Jobs

Figure 10.1 lists some future biotechnology and human augmentation jobs. While both fields will require that a high percentage of applicants have advanced degrees in fields such as biology, genetics, and biochemistry,

- CRISPR technician
- Genetics counselor
- Enhanced crop genetic designer
- Gene therapy business developer
- Human augmentation counselor
- Cybernetics lawyer
- Gene therapy scientist
- Medical geneticist
- CRISPR food preservation genetic specialist
- Extinct species revival specialist
- Computer-brain interface ethicist

*Figure 10.1 Some future biotechnology and human augmentation jobs*

---

[†] "Half Man, Half Circuit: Who Are the People Who Are Choosing to Become Cyborgs?" March 24, 2016. open.edu. www.open.edu/openlearn/health-sports-psychology/health/health-sciences/half-man-half-circuit-who-are-the-people-who-are-choosing-become-cyborgs (accessed May 16, 2022).

there should also be a significant number of jobs for people with nonscientific backgrounds.

## Careers in Biotechnology and Human Augmentation

The National Institutes of Health (NIH) has a website (genome.gov) that spells out a number of the career paths in this field. Besides lab-oriented jobs, genetics counselor is a growing area for people interested in advising patients about their health and about decisions they might need to make about adapting to genomic risk. The NIH points out that the genomics career path can take a number of different directions with jobs available in industry (pharmaceutical companies, startups, and entrepreneurial opportunities), educational institutions, government, and health care (health care providers or hospitals). Genomics is a growth area that is currently experiencing a severe shortage of trained job applicants. Demand for employees will likely continue to outstrip supply past 2030.

## Majors and Centers of Instruction

College students interested in this field often choose majors such as biology, genetics, microbiology, molecular biology, or chemistry. A few universities actually offer undergraduate degrees in genomics. The University of California's Davis branch offers a bachelor's degree in genomics and, interestingly enough, lists *career outcomes* for people with that degree as genetic counselor, biotechnologist, physician, research, and agricultural technologist. Arizona State University offers an online B.S. degree in Biological Sciences with a concentration in genetics, cells, and developmental biology. While most colleges offer undergraduate genetics courses, a few do genomics courses, often taught from a sociological perspective. In other words, these courses examine genomics in terms of its possible impact on society. Most major universities do offer master's and PhD programs in genetics and genomics, with Stanford and Harvard leading the way.

## Short-Term Learning Opportunities

There are a number of short-term learning opportunities in this field. One intriguing approach is a genomics bootcamp that includes an online

book and additional instruction through a YouTube channel: https://
genomicsbootcamp.github.iobook/.

Stanford and Harvard both offer online classes, as do Coursera (over
80 different courses) and Udemy. Many universities offer courses on this
topic through their extension programs. The Technical University of
Denmark offers a course through Coursera in Whole Genome Sequenc-
ing of Bacterial Genomes—Tools and Applications, while the University
of California's San Diego campus' extension division offers a specialization in bioinformatics. The University of California's Berkeley campus'
extension division offers a course on CRISPR and CRISPR-Cas9 in conjunction with the Innovative Genomics Institute. What is interesting is
that the course is described as a way for lawyers as well as others to learn
enough to interact with colleagues working in genomics.

## Validating Knowledge for Those Already in Careers

The best way for people already in the workforce to validate their knowledge in this field for the purposes of career changing is to pursue a certificate program. Coursera and Udemy both offer certificates in a variety
of genomic areas. For career changers with backgrounds in business
areas, there are courses that approach genomics from that direction. People wanting to transfer their marketing or product manager skills to a
genomics company would find those courses as well as a certificate that
provides an overview of the field very useful when it comes to convincing a genomics company that they have a nice mix of general experience
in their specialization as well as enough technical training to know all
the key concepts and terminology. Another option for those already with
degrees is to consider the University of Connecticut's 12-unit graduate
certificate in clinical genetics and genomics. The units are all transferable
to the university's graduate programs in health care genetics and genetic
counseling. Stanford has an online certificate program and indicates it is
ideal for people in any one of a dozen or so roles. Among the roles list
were "emerging technology leaders, strategists and venture capitalists who
trade within the scientific medical space; medical sales representatives,
new product teams, and directors, managers or administrators who work
in non-scientific roles in scientific environments."

# CHAPTER 11

# Nanotechnology

Nanotechnology consists of manipulating molecules and atoms to create new materials. We're talking about a world so small that it's hard to imagine. This technology creates objects that are measured in nanometers, one billionth of a meter or $10^{-9}$. Keep in mind that a strand of human hair is around 80,000 to 100,000 nanometers in diameter.* Famed physicist Richard Feynman first described this concept in a speech he gave at Caltech in 1959 with the title, *There's plenty of Room at the Bottom* in which he described using "machine-guided motion to assemble molecular structure with atomic precision."[1]

## U.S. Government Nanotechnology Initiatives

President Bill Clinton helped create the National Nanotechnology Initiative (NNI) back in 2000. Since its origin, the U.S. government has provided $38 billion dollars in support. Its mission is to ensure that the United States remains the leader in this field. In 2022, President Biden's budget proposes $1.98 billion to promote research and development to support the NNI. To that end, its goals include promoting the commercialization of this technology, providing the infrastructure for nanotechnology development, and engaging the public and ensuring there is an adequate work force in this area. Its website (www.nano.gov) provides the latest news on this topic as well as educational resources.

## Current Drivers of Nanotechnology

Besides the government's continuing support through its NNI, growth in this field is driven by environmental concerns, medical applications, and

---

* See www.nano.gov for more comparisons to illustrate just how small the world of nanotechnology is.

commercial manufacturing applications. Concern about climate change is driving research into how nanotechnology can preserve water as well as improve its quality as well as how it can provide relief for farmers whose crops are suffering from draught conditions. Medical applications represented the largest segment of the nanotechnology market in 2021, and the extensive research and development in this area is just now beginning to move to the stage of actual products.[†] Some emerging commercial manufacturing applications include food preservation and creating tennis balls that retain their bounce longer.

## Nanotechnology in Manufacturing

Research has led to the creation of nanotubes, one atom layer thick carbon structures that are excellent electrical conductors as well as extremely strong building blocks that can be used to strengthen everything from tennis racquets, surfboards, and ship turbines.[2] One very exciting area where real progress has been made is in the manufacturing of nanotechnology-based processors that make it possible to make even more powerful computers. Nanotechnology also has practical applications in the creation of batteries that provide far longer life. Nanotechnology in the form of sensors could prove to be a boon for the construction and transportation industries because these microscopic sensors could be used to monitor the structural integrity of bridges, parking structures, and rails as well as communicate with automobiles to ensure minimum congestion and prevent accidents caused by drivers veering into occupied lanes.[‡]

One very exciting area where real progress has been made is in the manufacturing of nanotechnology-based processors that make it possible to make even more powerful computers. Nanotechnology also

---

[†] "Nanotechnology Market, By Type (Nanosensors, Nanodevice, Nanomaterials, Others), By Application (Information Technology (IT), Homeland Security, Medicine, Transportation, Food Safety, Others), By End-use, and By Region Forecast to 2030." February 2022. emergenresearch.com. www.emergenresearch.com/industry-report/nanotechnology-market (accessed May 2, 2022).

[‡] Ibid.

has practical applications in the creation of batteries that provide far longer life.[§]

## Nanotechnology in Medicine and Health Care

This field offers great promise for nanotechnology. Embedded nano-sized sensors will be able to track various conditions, while nano-sized lasers will be able to focus on destroying cancer cells much more efficiently than current methods. Nanotechnology will be able to contribute to medical diagnosis and treatment as well as make imaging more efficient as well as creating lightweight strong prosthetics. Research is currently being conducted in using nanoparticles to mimic the behavior of *good* cholesterol to treat atherosclerosis by shrinking plaque.[¶]

## Nanotechnology in Food Science

Nanotechnology offers some very tangible advantages to the food science industry, including producing food that lasts far longer without spoiling. In addition, this technology could be used to create food containers that will keep insects out. Nano-encapsulated minerals and vitamins can enhance the quality of the food, while nano-encapsulation could also enhance flavor. Nano structured lipids can be used to mimic fats and thus create food that has the smoothness and creaminess of butter without needing fat.[3]

## Nanotechnology in the Aerospace Industry

Because nanotechnology can create incredibly strong materials that also are light, this technology lends itself to the aerospace industry. Boeing is using nanotechnology for creating lighter, stronger fuselage and wings for its Dreamliner 786.[4]

---

[§] Sell also "Nanotechnology Market by Type (Nanosensor and Nanodevice) and Application (Electronics, Energy, Chemical Manufacturing, Aerospace and Defense, Healthcare, and Others) Global Opportunity Analysis and Industry Forecast: 2021–2030." July 2021. alliedmarketresearch.com. www.alliedmarket research.com/nanotechnology-market (accessed May 2, 2022).

[¶] "Applications of Nanotechnology." n.d. www.nano.gov. www.nano.gov/about-nanotecvhnology/applications-nanotechnology (accessed May 2, 2022).

# Nanotechnology in Agriculture

Agriculture is an exciting area for nanotechnology research and development because of the need to counter the impact of climate change. Sensors placed in fields can provide data on the actual soil moisture levels. Nanotechnology is being used to develop nano-fertilizers and nano-pesticides.[5]

# Current Limitations to Nanotechnology Growth

There are a number of obstacles in the way of rapid growth of the nanotechnology industry. There is very little knowledge as yet on nanoparticles' possible harmful effect on humans. U.S. and EU regulators are investigating, but the field is still so new that it is difficult to develop safety regulations. A second limitation is the cost of equipment required to develop nanotechnology products. A third obstacle today is the shortage of nanotechnology-trained people. Finally, many of the possible uses of this technology require subjecting products to extreme conditions, whether that means harsh weather or other harsh environments. As normal materials change their properties so dramatically when reduced to the nanotechnology level, there is still a need to study such products carefully before going into production.

# Timetable for Explosive Growth

Research firms that track the nanotechnology industry are bullish on its growth. Allied Market Research forecasts a cumulative annual growth rate (CAGR) of 36.4 percent between 2021 and 2030 with the market growing to $33.63 billion by 2030.[**] Emergen Research forecasted this same period (2021–2030) to have a similar CAGR of 34 percent.[††]

---

[**] "Nanotechnology Market by Type (Nanosensor and Nanodevice) and Application (Electronics, Energy, Chemical Manufacturing, Aerospace and Defense, Healthcare, and Others) Global Opportunity Analysis and Industry Forecast: 2021-2030."

[††] "Nanotechnology Market, By Type (Nanosensors, Nanodevice, Nanomaterials, Others), By Application (Information Technology (IT), Homeland Security, Medicine, Transportation, Food Safety, Others), By End-use, and By Region Forecast to 2030."

- Medical nanobot specialist
- Nanotechnology agricultural consultant
- Nanotechnology security specialist
- Nanotechnology military applications specialist
- Nanotechnology battery enhancement specialist
- Nanotechnology chip designer

*Figure 11.1 Some future nanotechnology jobs*

Nanotechnology is moving from a research and development stage to a stage where it can produce *passive* products that, for example, strengthen existing material. As noted earlier, that might mean making a tennis racquet incredibly strong. Tameem Rahman, who characterizes himself as an "emerging tech and growth enthusiast," has studied the possible growth path of nanotechnology and sees a rapidly approaching second stage of development when nanotechnology produces *active* products that can perform functions and tasks. Further down the road is a third stage when nanotechnology can produce nano factories where they can product an item atom by atom and, finally, after a bit more time, perfect nanosystems that could produce items for virtually every field.[6] Figure 11.1 lists some of the future jobs nanotechnology likely will produce.

Arthur C. Clarke once wrote that any sufficiently advanced technology would be indistinguishable from magic. Such would likely be the case with nanotechnology by 2050 when virtually anything could be manufactured out of thin air using carbon, hydrogen, nitrogen, and so on at the atomic level. In the meantime, though, the period of 2022 to 2030 will likely move the nanotechnology field from the theoretical to the practical with passive and, likely, active products.

## Careers in Nanotechnology

The career opportunities in nanotechnology are enormous because nanotechnology applications impact so many different industries. The potential uses of this technology in the biomedical, computer electronics, and agriculture fields are obvious, but fields such as food science, textiles, security, energy, and chemicals also will need trained nanotechnology workers. While those interested in research or academic careers will need graduate degrees, there also will be a need for trained technicians as well as for support staff with skills in everything from public relations and technical writing to finance and marketing.

## Majors and Centers of Instruction

It is not necessary to major in nanotechnology for an undergraduate four-year degree, although a few schools now offer this option. The University of California's San Diego campus, Virginia Tech, SUNY Polytechnic Institute, Northwestern, Rice, and Louisiana Tech are among those that universities that do. Useful undergraduate majors include engineering, material science, chemistry, physics, and biology, depending on the industry students are interested in entering. The U.S. government's site on nanotechnology includes a place where students can research two-year degree programs by state (http:// nano4me.org/students). Many universities offer advanced degrees in material science and nanotechnology. The University of California's Riverside campus offers an online master's degree in nanotechnology engineering.

## Short-Term Nanotechnology Learning Opportunities

There are numerous online short-term learning opportunities available in the field of nanotechnology. www.classcentral.com listed over 50 online classes and over 30 certificate programs available in 2022. This website aggregates courses from a number of sources, including Coursera, so it is very useful place to start investigating classes and certificates.

## Validating Knowledge for Those Already in Careers

Clearly one of the certificate programs found at classcentral.com would help to validate knowledge of nanotechnology for those planning to change careers. For those already in technical fields, some of the short-term workforce training programs might help fill in gaps. The California Institute of Nanotechnology, for example, offers high-tech professional development training programs for people with technical skills who have lost their jobs: www.cinano.com.

# CHAPTER 12

# Emerging Technologies

I've reserved this chapter for emerging technologies that will require more time to reach maturity compared to the technologies I've previously discussed in this book. That doesn't mean that they are irrelevant when it comes to career considerations, especially since in the case of quantum computing, major corporations, including Google, Microsoft, and IBM, are already hiring personnel and expanding their research. As of this writing, IBM's research division already has over 4,000 employees with quantum computing as one of its major projects.[1] In fact, there are a number of startups in this field already, and career websites indicate that the demand for qualified people in this new field far exceeds the supply.

## Quantum Computing

Quantum computing is based on the quantum theory. Unlike conventional computers that work only with two possible states, a one or a zero, quantum computers utilize the equivalent of bits called qubits that can represent multiple degrees of ones and zeros states simultaneously. At the same time, in the strange world of quantum physics, there is entanglement of subatomic particles, in this case, qubits. What that means is that no matter how far apart they are, these particles correlate with each other, so the state of one particle can be determined by examining another particle. When more qubits are added to a quantum computer, there's a geometric increase in processing power and not just a linear increase. Unlike in a conventional computer where a programmer might have to try several different combinations of ones and zeroes to find the correct answer, a quantum computer can consider all these possibilities simultaneously as its qubits can function in both a state of zero and in a state of one. A quantum computer can perform calculations in seconds that might take conventional computer years to perform. As an example, soon after Google announced a breakthrough in performance of its quantum computer, China responded with an announcement of its own. Its quantum computer performed calculations in one hour that would have taken a conventional computer eight years to perform.[2]

### What Are Some Possible Applications for Quantum Computing?

IBM probably has the best handle on what applications are appropriate for quantum computing because their current corporate and government customers are the most likely candidates to use this technology as these customers need it and have the deep pockets to pay for it. The company has identified complex time-consuming computing applications in several industries. For the financial industry, it points to value-at-risk analysis, trading optimization, derivative pricing, fraud detection, and cred/asset scoring.*

With airlines, quantum computing applications include the untangling of operations disruption, enhancing contextual personalized service, and optimizing global network planning.† For the chemicals and petroleum industries, IBM is targeting the development of chemical products, expanding reservoir production, and optimizing feed stock routing and taking product to market.‡ Finally, for the biological sciences, IBM sees a match for applications such as creating precision medicine therapies by linking genomes and outcomes, improving patient outcomes by improving the enhancing the discovery of small molecule drug discover, and discovering novel biological products based on protein folding predictions.§ While IBM does not specifically mention it because it is not an application as far along in its development, quantum computing eventually will be using for encryption and for breaking encryption codes.

---

* "The Quantum Decade." June 10, 2021. ibm.com, p. 65. www.ibm.com/thought-leadership/institute-business-value/report/quantum-decade (accessed May 17, 2022).
† Ibid, p. 71.
‡ Ibid, p. 83.
§ Ibid, p. 94.

## Obstacles to Widespread Quantum Computer Adoption

Quanta interference remains a major issue at the moment as well as a determination of the ideal storage media for data. A startling announcement in 2021 about the possible use of photons in quantum computing may shorten the period until deployment.[3]

## Timeline for Quantum Computing

IBM estimates that quantum computing currently is where artificial intelligence was in 2010. In fact, Ilyas Khan, the founder and CEO of Cambridge Quantum Computing said that,

> In 10 years we will have achieved what took 40 to 50 years in classic computing... But by 2030, we will have figured out how businesses can use quantum computer—with no in-depth knowledge of how it actually works.[5]

## Future Jobs in Quantum Computing

Figure 12.1 lists some of the future jobs likely to be available in the quantum computer field. The majority of jobs will be technical in nature related specifically to hardware and software, there also will be a need to commercialize the products. That opens up the field to people who specialize in marketing, finance, and so on.

- Quantum computer programmer
- Quantum computer designer
- Quantum computer application specialist
- Quantum computing business developer
- Quantum computing algorithm developer
- Quantum computing quality control analyst

*Figure 12.1 Some future quantum computing jobs*

---

[5] Ibid, p. 53.

# Space Travel

The commercial push for space travel is growing exponentially. There will be all kinds of space-related jobs in the future, and not just for astronauts. It probably is not coincidental that the Colorado School of Mines already is offering a course as well as a certificate and master's and doctoral degrees in space resources. This field covers, among other topics, identifying resources in space, and figuring out how to collect, extract, and utilize them.** Industry watchers note that the space economy grew to $470 billion in 2020. Morgan Stanley Estimates this will be a trillion-dollar industry by 2040.[4]

### Private Companies Take the Lead in the United States

While several governments such as China and India have invested heavily in future space missions, the focus in the United States has been on private companies with some government support. Still, NASA's Artemis program has a goal of landing humans on the moon in 2025 to begin building a base camp. Several companies, including SpaceX, Blue Origin, and Virgin Galactic, have launched vehicles into orbit with future plans ranging from tourism to colonization of Mars. The sheer volume of launches is significant.[5] What once was science fiction is moving rapidly toward something very real. Among the topics under active discussion by national space programs as well as by the private companies mentioned previously are space tourism including space hotels (Obitalassembly.com), bases on the moon (China), a Martian colony (SpaceX.com), and asteroid mining (astidminingcorporation.co.uk). Elon Musk's SpaceX is developing what it calls the Starship system. When complete, it is expected to be capable of carrying up to 100 people to Mars.

### Obstacles to Success

The U.S. government has eliminated one of the major obstacles for this fledgling industry by deregulating restrictions that prevented people from

---

** See "Google Claims Quantum Supremacy." October 24, 2019. futuretime .net. www.futuretimeline.net/blog/2019/10/24.htm (Last visited May 17, 2022 and accessed May 18, 2022).

prospecting and harvesting resources in space. Asteroid mining is also open for private companies to drill. There are other obstacles that must be overcome. The cost of transporting goods and people into space is still a major obstacle. Fortunately, that cost has been dropping. Compared to 1970, using NASA's rockets to transport something into low earth-orbit costs 20 to 40 times less, depending on the rocket used.[††] What is really a game-changer is the concept of a space elevator that could drop the cost of transporting goods into space to around $100 per pound. While work on this stalled because of the lack of a material strong enough to handle the job, recent work on carbon nanotubes and graphene suggests that a solution is possible.[6]

Private companies are driven by a desire for profits, and this so far has not been possible. That might change, though as mining on the Moon and Mars as well as on asteroid begins. If water is discovered, hydrogen could be separated out. Lockheed Martin and Boeing both heavily invested in building the rockets used for space launches, created United Launch Alliance. It announced it will pay $500 per kilogram for fuel derived from water and supplied on the moon and $3,000 per kilogram for the same water-derived fuel supplied in low-earth orbit.[7]

## Timetable for Growth

Morgan Stanley's $1 trillion estimate for the space industry by 2040 seems possible. While SpaceX's timetable for Mars has slipped a bit, it has successfully landed and then relaunched its rockets, a key goal on the way toward a Mars colony. Interestingly enough, it is advances in another emerging technology (nanotechnology) that is pushing up the timetable for the creation of a space elevator, a real game-changer when it comes to making the cost of space transport low enough to make it profitable.

---

[††] An April 2020 market study by the consultancy Northern Sky Research forecast 140 missions to the moon over the next decade with an estimated expenditure of $42.3 Billion. "The 36th Annual Space Symposium Special Edition." 2021. swfound.org. https://swfound.org/media/207248/the-space-report-special-edition-features-on-lunar-development.pdf (accessed May 18, 2022).

- Space pilot
- Space travel tour guide
- Spaceship operations manager
- Space travel marketing specialist
- Asteroid mining specialist
- Colony agricultural specialist

- Space medicine doctor
- Space travel freight management
- Space travel lawyer
- Space flight insurance specialist
- Space travel lobbyist
- Colony designer
- Terraforming specialist
- Space engineer

*Figure 12.2  Some future space exploration jobs*

### Future Jobs in the Space Industry

Figure 12.2 lists some of the future jobs that should be available in the space industry. While many of these jobs likely will require science and math degrees, others have their counterparts in other industries but with a *space* flavor. So, for example, tour guides, hotel managers, lobbyists, and insurance specialists already exist. People with background in those jobs could add some specific knowledge of the space field and find themselves in demand.

# Fusion Energy

Fusion energy's benefits sound like a dream. Potentially, it offers a clean energy source that offers unlimited energy without any possibility of a Chernobyl-type accident. A new energy source would generate an enormous number of jobs that could not be outsourced. The devil is in the details of the physics behind fusion and what actually happens when the nuclei of small atoms stick together and fuse to release energy. This fusion creates electrically charged plasma that exists at temperatures higher than found on the Sun.

### Obstacles to Success

The most obvious obstacle that needs to be overcome is how to contain the plasma because it is so hot. There is hope on the horizon, though, because MIT scientists in conjunction with a spinoff called Commonwealth

Fusion Systems have designed a fusion plant that uses electromagnet technology to produce a magnetic field that is strong enough to contain the plasma. The optimistic forecast for this design is a working plant that can produce electricity within a decade.[8] That's a much more optimistic forecast than for the massive International Thermonuclear Experimental Reactor (ITER), which isn't even scheduled for completion until 2035 and was not designed to actually create electricity.

A second major obstacle to fusion energy becoming a viable source of clean energy is its enormous cost. Up until recently, the U.S. government has been supplying most of whatever limited funds fusion projects received. That is changing now. The Fusion Industry Association has more than 30 members, and 18 of these firms reported funding of more than $2.4 billion in 2021.[9]

## Reasons for Optimism

The U.S. Department of Energy has been leading the efforts to increase funding and speed up development of fusion technology. There is a political motivation as well. Recently, Kronos Energy issued a press release containing a picture of an American flag and the announcement that its fusion plant would generate lots of jobs in America that could not be outsourced to countries with cheaper labor. The fact that venture capital is now flowing to private fusion companies indicates that these investors have done their own risk/reward analyses and concluded that fusion energy is worth betting on. Finally, there is the motive of reducing carbon emissions from fossil fuel-based plants and fighting climate change. On that front, some environmentalists have argued that fusion plants will not be in operation soon enough to help meet the Paris climate change accords. Still, they do not oppose fusion energy but only want solar and wind firms to continue to receive government financial support.

## Timetable for Success

We should see meaningful progress in the development of fusion energy by the end of this decade. Certainly, by 2040, it should be a growing part of a country's energy source.

*Future Jobs in Fusion Energy*

Initially, the first jobs in fusion energy were technical in nature because much of the early work was theoretical in nature. Now there is a growing need for more hands-on workers, including those in construction. Once the plants have been constructed, jobs for people in the business side of the industry will open up. Figure 12.3 lists some future jobs in fusion energy.

# Careers in These Emerging Technologies

*Careers in Quantum Computing*

The fastest areas of growth for quantum computing, given its embryonic state, are engineers, research scientists, and software developers. Down the road, there will be a need for business-trained personnel, including developers, publicists, technical writers, marketing staff, and so on. Quantum computing will remain primarily the domain of scientists with advanced degrees for the next few years. The path toward careers in this field is reasonably clear.

*Majors and Centers of Quantum Computing Instruction*

The most appropriate majors at this time are in physics, mathematics, and computer science. While universities don't offer undergraduate degree in quantum physics, certainly physics majors can take elective courses in this area. Well-known universities offering graduate programs in quantum physics include MIT, Cal Tech, Harvard, Stanford, the University of California's Berkeley campus, and the University of Maryland.

*Short-Term Quantum Computing Learning Opportunities*

MIT offers an online two-course professional certificate in quantum computing. edX offers online courses in quantum computing as well as

- Nuclear fusion engineer
- Fusion plant construction project manager
- Nuclear fusion researcher
- Fusion plant designer
- Fusion marketing specialist
- Fusion business developer

*Figure 12.3 Some future fusion energy jobs*

quantum mechanics from several different universities, including UC Berkeley. Some are for those people with no previous knowledge of the field. Coursera also offers several courses, including quantum physics, taught by faculty from the University of Maryland. Classcentral.com listed over 50 courses in quantum computing, many of them free, on the day I surveyed that website. Stanford has offered and might offer again a six-week bootcamp on quantum computing in conjunction with engineers from IBM. Udemy.com offers an online bootcamp on quantum computing that starts with basics and then moves to more advanced topics. It is very inexpensive.

## Validating Knowledge for Those Already in Careers

MIT offers a few certificate programs in quantum computing, including one focused on business applications. The University of Rhode Island offers a graduate certificate program in quantum computing. For people already working in other areas of science and engineering, Stanford offers a nine-week online course in quantum mechanics for scientists and engineers. For people interested in learning to program quantum computing, Quiskit (https://quiskit.org) offers perhaps the most intriguing approach under its Learn tab. This company offers open-sourced software as well as a complete self-paced program to learn quantum computing

## Careers in the Space Industry

NASA astronaut candidates now require at least a master's degree in a space, engineering, or science field. Still, there will be a lot of space careers for those with undergraduate degrees. The career paths depend on areas of interest. For those who want to become pilots, the road leads through aeronautical engineering and actual flying experience either as a private pilot or a military pilot. Robotics engineers will be needed to handle robots used for exploration. Space medicine is an exciting career path as is exobiology. The space industry will need people in so many varied areas, including architects for designing habitats, colonists, 3D printing specialists to program, and then print what is needed in space, computer personnel to staff equipment, mining specialists, and material science specialists to mine for asteroids, and so on. For those interested in fields such as insurance, law, or logistics, imagine adding a specialization in space-related issues.

## Majors and Centers of Instruction

The Colorado School of Mines has jumped the gun by already offering a program in asteroid mining. Arizona State University has an entire School of Earth and Space Exploration and offers undergraduate certificates as well as minors. Many universities offer undergraduate degrees in astrophysics, aerospace engineering, electronic and mechanic engineering, and astronomy. While the well-known universities such as Cal Tech, MIT, Harvard, and Berkeley are well represented on any list of places to pursue advanced degrees for space exploration, schools you may never think of also offer sound programs. As an example, NASA is working closely with students from the following schools to test their experiments on the space station: The University of Delaware, University of Idaho, Montana State University, the University of Nebraska, and New Mexico State University.

## Short-Term Learning Opportunities

Embry-Riddle University offers a 12-unit online graduate certificate program in space operations. Coursera offers 10 different space courses, and edX offers a number of short-term courses.

## Validating Knowledge for Those Already in Careers

For those already in the workforce who have an undergraduate degree, Florida Institute of Technology offers a graduate certificate in commercial space studies. The State University of New Jersey offers a four-week online certificate titled *Analyzing the Universe*. Princeton University offers an online certificate program in astrobiology. edX offers an eight-week online course in space mission design and operations.

## Fusion Energy Careers

Initially, there is demand for people trained in nuclear physics and plasma physics as well as in material science. There will be jobs for engineers of all kinds, including mechanical, electrical, and nuclear. As plants begin to be built, construction personnel who have some training in nuclear facility construction will be at a premium. Once the plants are built, there will be a need for all kinds of backgrounds, including computer science, marketing, operations, public relations, business development, technical writing, and so on.

### Majors and Centers of Instruction om Fusion Energy

Among the most common majors are nuclear physics, mechanical engineering, and nuclear engineering. There also are career paths for computer science and materials science majors. Students with advanced degrees in plasma physics also have a career path. The University of California's Berkeley campus offers an undergraduate degree in nuclear engineering and graduate training in plasma and fusion science and technology. Idaho State University offers an Associate of Applied Technology degree in Energy Systems Nuclear Operation. Thomas Edison State University offers an undergraduate degree in nuclear energy engineering.

### Short-Term Fusion Energy Learning Opportunities

edX, Coursera, and Udemy all offer several short-term courses in fusion energy.

### Validating Knowledge for Those Already in Careers

Arizona State University offers an online graduate certificate program in nuclear power generation. Bismarck State College offers online courses that can lead to a certificate program in nuclear engineering. edX offers courses in nuclear energy and plasma physics.

# CHAPTER 13

# Developing a Career Plan

You can't guess the future. If you don't believe, it's futile to try to guess precisely what the future will be, just ask the many people who figured they'd get rich by trying to time the stock market's ups and down. It's unlikely anyone in the 1960s who wasn't writing science fiction could have predicted electric cars, iPhones, and personal computers. However, having said that, it is possible to look at current well-established technology trends and make some extrapolations that seem reasonable.

It is clear that automation as well as several emerging technologies will impact the job market. Its impact is already apparent in the financial industry. Ask bookkeepers who now must compete with simple software programs or financial analysts who find their numbers dropping as artificial intelligence (AI) software starts to perform many tasks once considered impossible for a machine. AI-based data analytics software is outperforming human analysts when it comes to discerning meaningful data patterns. So, while it is impossible to guess the future and all the inventions likely to come, it is possible to prepare to deal with some of these current automation trends.

So, people reading this book should not think they must major in a certain field to be employable in the future. Instead, they should focus on considering how emerging technologies might impact their chosen field and take measures to ensure they will be in a perfect position to take advantage when disruptive technologies change the nature of work. So, if students are interested in becoming lawyers, accountants, or teachers, they might consider how to enhance the prospects for their longevity in these professions. A law student might consider adding a specialization in AI law or blockchain smart contracts; an accounting student might want to add a specialization in blockchain or green accounting, while students planning to become teachers might want to become comfortable with augmented reality and 3D printing. People considering careers in marketing might want to take some courses in AI and the use of data analytics. People interested in food science might want to explore future applications of nanotechnology as well as the use of 3D printers to *print* food. Agriculture majors might want to learn something about the use of sensors to monitor crop soil as well as agricultural applications of gene editing. They certainly will want to learn about what is required for sustainable agriculture.

## A Degree Versus Lifelong Learning

What is perfectly apparent already is that universities and high schools are ill equipped to prepare students for the world of work. No one should believe that what he or she learns in a four-year college degree program will be adequate or even relevant a decade or so after graduation. It is likely that employees will need to accept the need for lifelong education as a requirement if they wish to stay employable. That does not mean leaving the workforce for significant time while going back to a university for an additional degree. Rather, it means short, intense doses of learning that can update skills or provide a validation of new skills necessary to remain employable.

## Not Everyone Need Become a Scientist or Engineer

I've tried to emphasize in the chapters on emerging technologies that there will be jobs for people who did not choose to earn science or engineering degrees. The companies that sell products based on these new technologies will still need to staff traditional departments like human resources, finance, marketing, and operations. There are plenty of short-term learning opportunities for people in these disciplines to gain enough familiarity with these new technologies to be valuable assets to their companies.

## Coping Strategies for Preparing for the Onslaught of Robots and AI

Given the buying plans corporate executives reveal in surveys, the amount of money and planning going into deploying AI and robots is so considerable that it is becoming a raging river rather than a mere stream. With that in mind, I want to return to the metaphor I used earlier in this book where I likened the situation workers face today with the *invasion* of AI and robots to a war. So, let's examine different approaches workers can take.

### Ignoring the Invasion

This head-in-the-sand approach might help avoid some anxiety initially, but it is bound to lead to unemployment and the real possibility of being unemployable. Think of people in Europe during the late 1930s that chose to tell themselves that war was not imminent and Germany surely wouldn't start a world war. Magical thinking doesn't solve any problems.

### Flourishing as the Brains Behind the Robots and AI

Just as invading forces chose to protect and preserve the lives of those residents who had needed skills, manufacturers of robotic hardware and AI software will need specialists behind the scenes such as software developers, mechanical engineers, electrical engineers, AI specialists, user-interface specialists, Big Data analytics specialists, mechanics to keep robots running, and security specialists to keep AI data safe. These are just some of the jobs that already exist. In a later section, we'll examine the lengthy list of future jobs these new technologies will create.

### Working With the Robots

I used the metaphor of *collaborators* in my invasion metaphor earlier in the book. This coping measure will probably impact more workers than any other and involves working with robots collaboratively. I explained in Chapter 2 the concept of cobots, robots specifically designed to work with people without accidentally hurting them. To broaden the metaphor a bit, this coping mechanism includes working collaboratively with AI software as well as with machines.

Most studies reaffirm the idea that robots generally can only perform a certain percentage of the tasks that a worker assigned to a job normally performs. While that doesn't necessarily mean a 1:1 robot replacement for every worker, it does mean that some jobs will need to be performed collaboratively where the robot performs the tasks that it is handles effectively while the worker performs the tasks that humans excel at doing. As an example, a cobot's AI software can plan the most efficient pick list at a warehouse. A human worker can accompany this cobot on the most-efficient route to where an item is stored and then use his or her much more sensitive hands to actually pick up the object and place it on the cobot for transport.[1]

The close collaboration between human and cobot is going to get a lot closer. Researchers believe that before long, it will be possible to use a brain–computer interface for a human worker to communicate directly to a cobot in language it can understand.[2] That's just another example of a human collaborating with a robot, in this case by using an emerging technology discussed in Chapter 12.

### Managing the Robots and AI Software

Entrepreneurs and those interested in management careers will want to understand enough about emerging technologies to be able to make intelligent business decisions about their use. There are a growing number of executive management courses and certificate programs that offer a managerial perspective on deploying new technology in the most cost-effective and efficient ways. Department managers also fit into this category. When the CEO decides to deploy AI in the finance department, its manager can become an enthusiastic volunteer and facilitate the implementation or resist, actively or passively, and then pay the consequences. The same principle applies to a high school or elementary school administrator when the Superintendent decides to adopt a virtual reality-based curriculum for social studies or even a college basketball coach at a university where the athletic director decides to deploy analytics to get a better handle on what works and doesn't work on the basketball court.

### Going Where Robots Can't Follow

Another coping mechanism for humans is to carve out careers in areas that place a premium on human skills. Robots and AI are not empathetic.

Humans expect that skill in people they interact with in areas that require that emotion. Some examples of careers where empathy is necessary include nurse, trainer or coach, psychologist, financial advisor, lawyer, doctor, interior designer, accountant, and HR managers. If you add the requirement for good communications skills, you might include project managers and graphic designers.*

We also are far from the point where robots could replace a CEO or department manager because humans are not ready to take orders or be evaluated by nonhumans. Robots and AI are also far from ready to replace humans in sophisticated sales jobs. So much of that job's success is based on human relations skills, the ability to relate to and communicate with a customer on a personal level, and the ability to understand body language and what is unsaid. I remember, for example, the time I visited the key decision maker in a global Fortune 100 company. An associate warned me to be sure to find a way to sit down with her when discussing my product. I soon realized why. The decision maker was more than a foot shorter and female. Human psychology made it abundantly clear to my associate from past experience that this woman did not like having someone towering over her, even though that person wasn't making any deliberately threatening move. Another time an account executive warned me that the decision maker was very vain, and I should be sure to ignore anything I might find amusing. Sure enough, this high-level executive walked in after a break in his day for swimming with the very few strands of hair he still had combed over his head in a way that would have gotten a smile out of me if I hadn't been warned.

Let me give you one final example of how a sophisticated salesperson can rise to a level that a robot could never achieve. My company had designated a single named account for this account executive, and his quota was well over a million dollars' worth of business. Despite some hard times for that company, its senior executives always warmly welcomed him, and he always met or exceeded his quota. I noticed that he kept a small notebook with him and wrote notes during casual conversation

---

* "12 Jobs That Robots and AI Will Replace in the Future and 12 That Won't." October 5, 2021. saviom.com. www.saviom.com/blog/12-jobs-that-robots-ai-will-replace-in-the-future-and-12-that-wont/ (accessed May 18, 2022).

with his customers. He also met with some of these executives after hours to play tennis and go out for cocktails. One day I accompanied him into the office of a very high-level executive. They exchanged pleasantries and then my colleague dropped a bombshell. He asked if the executive had heard about an upcoming major reorganization. This man's face dropped, and he shook his head and then encouraged my colleague to fill him in. In other words, my colleague knew the inside scoop about a major company's internal machinations better than this company's senior executive.

Another area where automation is very likely never to enter is that of the craftsman. I know someone, for example, who is constantly creating new types of jewelry that she sells online. She seems to find inspiration every day to create new color combinations. Someone else I know creates beautiful vases that are works of art. Each one is unique. Because so much of craftsmanship consists of creating limited volumes of a number of different objects, it is not really cost-effective or practical to use robots that way. Also, robots never have been known for their creativity. So, artists of all types, musicians, and craftspeople are likely in niches that manufacturers of robots likely will find financially unattractive markets for their products.

Yet another area where robots and AI are not likely to be successful for quite a while is in professions that deal with areas where people lack knowledge or confidence. One example is cryptocurrency. It is such a new area that most people over 30 want to talk to a real broker and not a software program to address any concerns they might have. You can add genetic counselors, consultants, personal trainers, and life trainers to the list of careers where a personal relationship with clients is important. Most people also still want to talk to a realtor when buying or selling their homes, although that might change in the distant future when the buyer and seller might negotiate together and agree on a smart contract on a blockchain.

## What Are the Human Skills Robots Can't Match?

There still will be a demand for unique human skills. McKinsey consultants have forecast the impact of automation on jobs. They surveyed corporate executives and discovered that while they did prize coding skills and other technical skills, they estimated demand for social and emotional skills would grow across all the industries by 26 percent in the United States and 22 percent in Europe.[3]

Among the human or *soft skills* generally mentioned where humans are superior to robots are empathy, critical thinking, adaptability, communication, and creativity.[4] Other soft skills researchers often mention include sociability, curiosity, problem-solving, persuasiveness, flexibility, and conscientiousness. Interestingly enough, the U.S. Bureau of Economic Research published a study that managed to quantify the value of some of these soft skills.[5]

## Do You Have the *Soft Skills* Needed for Future Employment?

Many of the *soft skills* that human workers can utilize to differentiate themselves from robot workers can be categorized as emotional intelligence. Howard Gardner defined a number of different types of human intelligence in his landmark book, *Frames of Mind: The Theory of Multiple Intelligences*.[6] While he described human intelligence associated with music, dance, and athletics (kinesthetic), linguistic, as well as several other types, it was Daniel Goldman who coined the term *emotional intelligence* a decade later.[7] It turns out that researchers have developed a test to determine a person's emotional intelligence. The Mayer–Salovey–Caruso Emotional Intelligence Test (MSCEIT) contains 141 items and is comprised of eight tasks, two per each of the four emotion abilities (perception/expression of emotion, use of motion to facilitate thinking, understanding of emotion, and management of emotion in oneself and others). It is possible to take this test free online.[†] If this seems like too arduous a task, two researchers have published a book that includes a much less complex validated test.[8]

If you need help in improving your emotional intelligence, there are online courses and even certificate programs to validate this skill. Udemy offers a number of classes and certificates, including *The Complete*

---

[†] You can take the test at this website: https://globalleadershipfoundation.com/geit/eitest.html (accessed May 18, 2022).

*Emotional Intelligence Masterclass* taught in conjunction with LinkedIn Learning. Coursera offers several courses and certificates that include courses taught by faculty at the University of Michigan and the University of California's Davis campus. edX offers a course taught by faculty from the University of California's Berkeley campus. There are other online options as well, including courses from Cornell University and Harvard.

Remember that there are a number of skills and not just emotional intelligence under the category of *soft skills*. Critical thinking and creativity are two key skills often mentioned when discussing what corporations want in their employees. As it might be difficult to demonstrate those skills in certain jobs or it might seem very subjective, once again, there are courses and certificates to validate these skills. Coursera has a number of online courses in critical thinking, including an intriguing offering from Cambridge University as well as courses from Cornell and Duke. As far as creativity training goes, Harvard has an online certificate program in creative thinking, while Coursera offers 10 different courses at the time I'm writing this chapter. Udemy offers a number of online classes, including an intriguing one titled *Master Class—Creative Problem Solving and Decision Making*.

## Use the O*NET to Match Skills and Interests

Whether someone is a student or someone already in the workforce who would like to change careers or augment his skills and knowledge to take advantage of opportunities provided by emerging technologies, the U.S. government's *Occupational Information Network* or O*NET is available online at onetonline.org. At the time I'm writing this chapter, this database contains information on 923 different occupations. It is possible to search this database by skills required, type of work, and by the 277 descriptors collected on each occupation. There's an excellent video available to explain this marvelous tool.[‡]

The O*NET Resource center page has a free Interest Profiler assessment tool to help people measure six different types of occupational interest they might have. From the main page, it is possible to do a search based

---

[‡] www.onetcenter.org/programvideos.html#overview (accessed May 18, 2022).

on your *soft* skills and one based on your technical skills. You can search by location of the country to examine opportunities in certain fields. If you are already in the workforce, you can plug in your current job duties and see what other jobs and fields need someone with that kind of experience. You also can examine what technology is now considered *hot* as well as what different industries have jobs that utilize that technology.

## Develop a Career Plan With Timelines

If you ever read Benjamin Franklin *Autobiography,* you might remember that he designed a systematic approach to improve himself. He listed several aspects of himself he wanted to work on and then assigned himself goals to work on each week. That's not a bad way to handle a large goal that at first glance might seem overwhelming. I'm making the assumption that the goal of most people reading this book is to ensure that they can build some career security and enhance their value as a current or future employee by preparing for the impact of emerging technologies. Whether someone is currently in college or in the workforce, it is a good idea to develop a career plan with timelines to ensure they can meet those goals. There should be a number of short- and long-term goals, including a completion date for achieving these tasks. So, here are some items you might want to include:

- Assess *soft* skills. If already in the workforce, check to see if any performance evaluations highlight your ability to collaborate, think outside the box, and so on.
- Take one of the credential courses to validate these skills.
- Use the O*NET to zero in on which *hot* technologies impact your career field.
- Locate short-term credential courses to validate your ability to be a leader when an emerging technology is deployed at your company.
- If you are already a manager, find a short-term program to validate your ability to be part of the upcoming technology deployment at your company.
- If you are in school, consider broadening your future employability, no matter what your major by carefully

choosing a minor and electives that provide some technical expertise. As an example, someone major in accounting might consider taking courses such as blockchain accounting or green accounting. Someone major in history with a desire to go to law school might want to consider learning more about smart contracts or AI.

## Preparing for a New Career or Career Change

It is never too soon to find a group of people in your vicinity who share the same interest in a technology or career field. Some of the members will already be working in that field and can provide valuable information as well as serve as key contacts.

A second option is to plan on attending a major trade show in the technology area that interests you. These enormous conventions provide the opportunity to hear about the latest trends and issues. Even more important, though, is the chance to visit the vast number of booths manned by staff from the leading companies in the field as well as from startups. There you can sit through demos about specific products and also question the staff about opportunities in the field. You can pick up business cards and establish connections that can lead to introductions to key decision makers.

While I certainly don't expect you to build a nanotechnology lab in your home, it is possible in the case of many of the emerging technologies to get some first-hand experience with them. That's certainly true with 3D printers because courses are available at many public libraries and community colleges. It is also possible to purchase an inexpensive 3D printer and begin learning the technology first-hand. In the case of virtual reality, it also is possible to purchase products and gain hands-on experience. Even buying a very small amount of a cryptocurrency can help when it comes to understanding blockchain technology.

## Research Is the Key to Success

As a former research director, I've always been very high on the value of research. The truth is that when it comes to planning a future career or planning to change careers, very few people take the time and effort to do adequate research on the opportunities these fields offer. Let's assume you have examined the technologies in this book and considered whether you really want to pursue a career in one of these technologies or try to bullet-proof your career to ensure that you can survive any deployment of these technologies. If you want to pursue one of the technologies discussed, then it's time to research which companies are leaders in that technology as well as where they are headquartered. Consider doing the following research:

- Begin by using a search engine to list the major companies in a particular technology field. Record their URLs as well as their location. Ask yourself if you are willing to move for a job and where you would like to live.

- Now explore the career opportunities section of these companies' websites. Begin collecting job descriptions of positions listed. What you should do at this point is to build a profile of the ideal candidate from these companies' perspectives.

- Once you have a pretty detailed profile, look at your own resume and work history. How do you match up? Now make a list of skills you don't have. Once you know where you are lacking, research online programs that offer ways of validating the skills and knowledge you currently lack.

- Make a timeline that lays out a schedule for filling in these gaps. If most VR companies require their job candidates to have a certain programming language, then look for classes or a bootcamp that can bring you up to speed.

- Attend tradeshows now with the express purpose of visiting the booths of the key companies you have identified as your top candidates. Consider that many of them don't advertise online but use recruiters. What you want to do is spend time with some of the staff at these booths and learn how to contact the key decision makers.

- Some technology companies offer classes for their customers as well as for the public. If one of the companies you've pinpointed does so, consider taking these classes. As a value-added reseller of networking products several years ago, I made it a point to take all the classes the company I was interested in offered. It turned out that doing so led me to a new career field where I spent many happy years. Another time, I made it a point to make contact with the department head for a Fortune 100 company. We had lunch and then he led me to the HR department where he told some very unhappy bureaucrats to hire me, even though I didn't have an application on file. I'm not saying that happens very often, but it did happen to me once. Another time, I met a manager at a trade show booth, and he wound up hiring me.

## College Students Should Look for Career Guidance Early

Some people start college unsure of a major. They stumble along until a course catches their interest. Think how haphazard that approach is! What if by chance a course with an award-winning professor is closed, while the same course taught by a graduate student without any interest in the topic is wide open? It's doubtful that the student will have the same excitement of majoring in that subject if he doesn't happen to take the section with the star teacher. I entered college with a premed major in chemistry because I liked the idea of becoming a doctor. Keep in mind I never knew any doctors personally or what their daily life was like. I realized later when I actually attended medical school that it wasn't the right career for me. I traded my pursuit of an MD for a PhD and never really regretted that decision. So, researching a field before you get too far into it is a very good idea. There are many articles on an average day in the life of someone in a particular field. Read over what these people enjoy doing. Does it sound appealing to you?

## Career Aptitude Tests Narrow Down Majors and Career Options

University career centers offer a variety of aptitude tests. If a student does not have any driving interest in a field, finding the time and effort to take some aptitude tests is very worthwhile. I remember taking some of these tests and being told that the one area I shouldn't pursue was engineering because I lacked spatial awareness. Ask me to imagine an object on a page turned around and I draw a blank. Fortunately, college career centers offer a variety of career aptitude tests. People already in the workforce should remember that their career centers usually offer them the same opportunity to take these tests. Many of these tests can also be taken online.

One of the most popular career assessment tools is the MAPP test that takes 22 minutes to complete (www.assessment.com). MAPP stands for Motivational Appraisal Personal Potential, and it matches your results against 1,000 possible careers. You do have to pay around $120 for a 22-page written analysis. I imagine that if you take this test through your career center, it probably covers that fee. The Myer–Briggs Type Indicator (MBTI) test is one of the most popular with companies that want to ensure your personality and interests will match their jobs. While there is a free version available online (humanmetrics.com), the paid version (myersbriggs.org) runs around $50. Finally, I mentioned the O*NET Profiler earlier. It is an excellent tool to match interests, skills, and possible jobs.

# CHAPTER 14

# Coping With Massive Change

The future is already here when it comes to automation. Bain and Company's analysts studied their crystal balls and concluded that automation might eliminate 20 to 30 percent of current jobs, particularly those of middle- to low-income workers, by the end of the 2020s. The result would be that the country's anemic demand growth would constrain economic expansion. They also predicted that growing levels of wealth inequality and market imbalances could trigger a reassessment of government's role in the marketplace.*

Analysts are not the only ones concerned about the impact of automation. When the Pew Research Center interviewed people and asked them about the impact automation would have on them in the future, many expressed concerns about being permanently unemployed or, at best, forced into lower paying service jobs. They also worried that the country's educational system was inadequately preparing people for the workplace of the future, and that economic and political institutions also would be poorly equipped to make the hard choices automation would require.[1]

That's quite an indictment of the institutions charged with protecting its citizens from the ravages of automation. Yet, that sentiment has been echoed by a number of experts who have already started worrying about the future. In this chapter, I'll look at early attempts by some of our various institutions to prepare for massive change as well as some prescriptions that might be needed to cure a broken system. Unfortunately,

---

* See Chapter 3 in K. Harris, A. Kimson, and A. Schwedel. February 7, 2018. *Labor 2030: The Collision of Demographics, Automation and Inequality*, bain.com. www.bain.com/insights/labor-2030-the-collision-of-demographics-automation-and-inequality/ (accessed April 25, 2022).

change does not come easily to institutions because inertia means that it is like trying to change the Queen Mary's course when it's already going full speed in the wrong direction.

## Changing Educational Institutions

Joseph Aoun is the President of Northeastern University, a school known for its innovative fifth-year internship programs. Students graduate with practical experience in fields related to their majors that improve their chances of companies hiring them. He points out that K-12 schools are focusing on teaching convergent rather than divergent thinking, and that convergent thinking is the type of thinking that robots can do extraordinarily well. The focus, he believes, should be on teaching creativity. Schools, he points out, are still based on this country's needs in the 19th and 20th century to develop factory workers by plying them with the type of information (or *hard skills*) that might prove useful for that type of work rather than the *soft skills* that are uniquely human.[2]

What about teaching creativity? Is that even possible? Erik Brynjolfsson and Andrew McAfee believe that early education seems to have an enormous impact on people's ability to think creatively. They point to the Montessori schools' self-organizing environment and hands-on learning approach as a way to teach children skills. Interestedly enough, it turns out that the founders of Google, Amazon, and Wikipedia all attended these schools.[3] It's not strictly an either/or choice because it is entirely possible that more traditional preschools and elementary schools could adopt some of these approaches without adopting the entire template and curriculum. After all, one of the weaknesses of the Montessori approach compared to traditional schooling is a lack of socialization. As many experts point to collaboration as a necessary human skill, schools would have to balance collaboration with self-organizing approaches.

A Stanford study predicted that while formal education in grades K-12 would not disappear, online education will take on a larger role. It also pointed to more student interaction with artificial intelligence both in the classroom and in the home. The use of virtual reality will mean that students will engage in more active learning experiences. Imagine students in the near future strolling through ancient Rome or Greece while studying history or observing the Founding Fathers' debates while creating the Constitution.[4]

Some social scientists suggest that preparing students to deal with the threat of automation should start as early as elementary school. They urge more focus on teaching technical skills such as coding and statistics as well as developing the more human skills of creativity and collaboration.[5] This would be true for all students, not just the ones on a fast track to careers in science and technology.

Many experts urge that vocational education should supplement a high-school's curriculum in conjunction with local career centers. The Tri-Rivers Career Center has developed a program that offers free enrollment for high-school students at RAMTEC. They earn their high-school diplomas while learning skills that local Ohio companies such as Honda and Robot Works demand when they hire workers.[6]

Some high schools have teamed with community colleges and businesses to create the equivalent of many of the vocational apprenticeship programs found in Europe. In Charleston, South Carolina, six employers partnered with a local technical college and the chamber of Commerce to create a program where high-school students work part-time during summers while taking math and science courses as well as technical coursework at that college. The high-school students aged 16 to 18 earn a year's credit toward a two-year associate's degree and then are hired by the participating firms.[7]

Higher education will require a thorough change. Aoun has thought deeply about the ways in which higher education needs to change, and he suggests that universities focus on four types of cognitive capacities: critical thinking, systems thinking, entrepreneurship, and cultural ability. He spells out how professors in various disciplines would incorporate this approach in their lectures.[†]

Aoun's approach would be a radical change as it would require integrating different disciplines, modifying teaching approaches, and changing the ways professors evaluate their students. I can't help but remember an aging tenured professor in a department where I taught who used his

---

[†]  See Chapter 3 in J.E. Aoun. *Robot-Proof: Higher Education in the Age of Artificial Intelligence.*

ancient lecture notes to deliver lectures for the same courses for more than two decades. One day, he dropped these notes during a lecture and couldn't recover and wing it. He had to dismiss the class early. While he clearly is not typical, I know for a fact that many professors take any attempts to tell them how to teach very personally and pride themselves on their academic freedom. Like piloting the Queen Mary, changing course for higher education will not be fast or smooth, regardless of the sense of urgency some educators feel. As a former university professor, I am well aware that the reward system is based on research and publications and not on teaching. I observed at one highly ranked university where I was an administrator that professors in a department where one of their own had been awarded a best teaching citation pointed to it as proof he was spending too much time on his teaching and not enough time on his research and were reluctant to promote him.

Our nations' community colleges are more likely to be where workers go for rapid vocational training. While a number of these schools reduced their vocational offerings when there was a push toward a more academic curriculum a few years ago, now the emphasis is shifting back toward a vocational emphasis but now with more of a business partnership. This approach benefits the college (more relevant curriculum), the students (more job opportunities), and businesses (better trained students able to jump right into jobs without a lot of additional training required). Siemens has teamed with a community college in North Carolina to train apprentices for its wind turbine factory in Charlotte. The program allows workers to *earn and learn* at the same time.[‡]

Perhaps less emphasis needs to be placed on the term *junior college* as the major purpose in the future is likely not to be to prepare students to transfer to universities to complete four-year degrees. The term *community college* better suits the role these educational institutions will play when it comes to preparing students for rapidly shifting job requirements.

---

[‡] "Re-educating Rita: Artificial Intelligence Will Have Implications For Policymakers in Education, Welfare, and Geopolitics." June 23, 2016. economist.com. www.economist.com/special-report/2016/06/23/re-educating-rita (accessed on April 25, 2022).

An MIT study of the impact of automation suggests that community colleges integrate their remedial educational classes and their vocational training rather than making them sequential. It also proposed the creation of shorter classes that could be used to provide usable credentials on the path to a degree and more financial support over shorter intervals so that adults could focus on their studies and not have to go part-time while they work.[8]

Some community colleges have been very proactive in their training initiatives. Rather than wait for businesses to approach it, Sinclair College in Dayton, Ohio, develops curricula and trains students in state-of-the-art fields and then uses this trained workforce to lure companies to settle there. One example cited by Ellen Ruppel Shell is the creation of a tool and die program, followed by the luring of a tool and die company to settle in Dayton.[9]

That's not to say that college students shouldn't also be exposed to a more academic study of data. Many automation experts argue that most students should be taught some coding even if they are likely never to have to code as part of their jobs. One reason is that often people will be in positions where they will have to work with programmers and make decisions based on what programmers tell them about the scope of projects. Knowing the language and basics of coding will help them make better decisions. Also, it will be many years before computers will be able to do their own complete coding. Programmers will still be in demand for many decades.

## Lifelong Education Will Become a Must

Automation will speed up as various technologies mature, and it will soon infringe on jobs once considered safe from the first wave of AI and robotic-driven automation. What that means is that workers in the near future will not be able to rely on what they learned in college to protect their jobs; they will have to retool themselves frequently through lifelong education. That does not mean going back to college to earn new degrees. Rather, as the founder of Udacity points out, it means *nano-degrees*, taking a short series of classes while already working and earning certificates that attests that the student acquired a certain set of skills and knowledge.

A number of companies and universities have sprung up to offer this type of short training.[§]

A Brooking's report recommends that students receive strong general training in *21st century skills* whenever they receive occupation- or industry-specific training. It also states that when these displacements do occur, more robust models of *lifelong learning* must be available for these workers to provide them with better retraining options than now exist. In the meantime, there should be temporary income support in the form of unemployment and wage insurance.[10]

Perhaps, lifelong learning retraining options could be speeded up. Some argue that educators should utilize artificial intelligence learning bots to help re-educate and upskill workers before they are laid off. Such bots could automate some of the curriculum and even match workers and their skills to new job opportunities.[11]

## Growing Social Unrest: A Prescription for Disaster

America is growing older. Demographers forecast that each year, the average age of Americans increases. That means, when automation really hits, there will be a sizable number of older people who will be retired and are likely to require government support. Today, less than half of people aged 65 to 74 have a retirement account.[12] Baby Boomers on the average have only saved enough to last them around seven years according to a study conducted by Charles Schwab.[13] Older Americans as a group purchase fewer goods. As the American economy is based on consumer consumption, the convergence of fewer people working, people retiring, and living longer due to breakthroughs in medical science, and large numbers of younger unemployed workers could create a situation where the country's economy winds up in free fall.

The U.S. economy cannot remain above water if a declining middle class reduces its spending. Think of all the jobs impacted when retail sales dry up. These jobs would not be limited to retail sales positions, but would also include people in positions such as buyers, marketers, distributors, truck drivers, payroll clerks, and shipping personnel. If those

---

[§] Ibid.

people lost their jobs, the impact would cascade as they in turn would spend less money for food, clothing, and housing. They likely would put off vacations and decide not to buy a new car.

Those decisions would impact still more people as the new car salesman decides his daughter will need to go to a community college rather than attend the local university. University administrators would find certain classes lack sufficient numbers of students, so they would cut faculty positions. The cascading impact is much like the impact on a lake when someone throws a stone into it. The ripples spread far and wide.

To compound that problem, keep in mind that the government will likely have less revenue in the future because nontaxpaying robots will replace a number of workers who did pay taxes. On top of that, the already sizable gap between haves and have-nots is likely to grow even greater as digital-savvy elites take well-paying jobs directing automation efforts and programming robots and AI systems while the ranks of unemployed grow. Brynjolfsson and McAfee point out that when new technology creates jobs, it tends to benefit the highly educated and thus creates clear winners and losers.[1]

A restive population of unemployed is a disaster just waiting to happen, so some social scientists are already looking for solutions. As robots assume most menial jobs and improve to the point that they can perform far more sophisticated jobs, a government probably will not be able to do what President Franklin Roosevelt did to quell the depression by creating make-work jobs. The problem is that massive unemployment caused by automation is not a temporary situation that can be papered over by paying people to work on government projects for the short term until the economy improves and new jobs are once again available.

Simply offering to re-educate unemployed workers will not work as there won't be enough lucrative fields still limited to human workers. As an example, imagine if unemployed coal miners are told they can be retrained to drive trucks, a traditional career move today for people with limited education. Driverless trucks controlled by AI software would make that career change impossible in the future. What about training

---

[1] See Chapter 10 in E. Brynjolfsson and A. McAfee. 2014. *The Second Machine Age: Work, Progress, and Prosperity in a Time of Brilliant Technology.*

people to teach? Robotic teachers are not that far beyond the horizon. They offer unlimited patience and cannot be unionized and demand higher wages.

Instead of solutions that might have worked in previous years, government advisors in the near future will need to be far more innovative when it comes to coming up with a way for middle-class people to have the income to drive the economy. Such solutions might call into question the long-term viability of capitalism in an age of automation.

## Providing Universal Basic Income (UBI)

Today, this country's voters are highly polarized politically. While the last few years have seen a conservative wave, the country historically has alternated between the two ideologies every few decades. The traditional conservative viewpoint that people need to rely on their own self-reliance to pull themselves *up with the bootstraps* is likely to give way to a more liberal position that people should expect their government to help them in a time of need in light of millions of people unemployed or underemployed.

According to economist Robert Reich, the Obama administration floated a proposal for wage insurance. Although it did not go anywhere, the idea might be resurrected in the future. The government could administer such a program by providing a worker who loses a $20 per hour job and can only find a $10 per hour job with enough funds to make up the difference.[14] Such a program might be enormously expensive, but it would probably prevent a lot of home evictions and homelessness, but would conservatives accept such a government intrusion into the private marketplace?

Another possible solution to deal with rising unemployment caused by automation that has been floated by economists is a universal basic income (UBI). Citizens would be entitled to a certain stipend. They would not be penalized if they found employment and chose to work in much the same way today that people who have reached 66 years of age are not penalized if they work while drawing social security paychecks. The argument that would be given to conservatives is that strict rules and safeguards would be put in place to limit stipends to citizens and not undocumented workers.

Citizens would likely spend their UBI funds for the basics of food, housing, transportation, and so on. Doing so would quickly put the money back into circulation and stimulate the economy much the way that a tax cut for the poorest Americans historically has resulted in a positive jolt to the American economy.

In order for UBI to work, though, the United States likely would have to offer free health care for all citizens; otherwise, the UBI, no matter how high, would not work because of high medical expenses. Europe obviously is well ahead of the United States because it already has a one-payer system in place.

## Early Supporters and Experiments

Support is growing for UBI. Mark Zuckerberg, Elon Musk, and Richard Branson have all argued that government must provide citizens with a *cushion* to address the loss of income due to automation. The range of UBI financial support currently being discussed is around $660 to $1,000 per month. The supposition is that citizens could then find satisfying work without as much concern for what it paid as their basic income requirements would be provided. It is interesting that European countries are far more likely to embrace UBI sooner than the United States because of the EU's historical liberal policies regarding social benefits.

Y Combinator has been conducting feasibility studies on basic income and will expand to a test involving two states and 3,000 people. Two groups will be given different amounts of income monthly ($50 for one group and $1,000 for the second group) to see how both groups react to UBI. The company wants to learn if a basic income will cause some people to become more entrepreneurial or take innovative risks as some of their costs are covered. Finland is conducting a major UBI experiment and is offering citizens around $700 a month, while Italy and Canada are also conducting tests.[**]

Stockton California ran an experiment where it provided 125 citizens with $500 a month. The mayor told an interviewer that this money often

---

[**] See "Re-educating Rita: Artificial Intelligence Will Have Implications for Policymakers in Education, Welfare and Geopolitics."

was the difference between eviction and homelessness and wants the program increased so that it can be offered to a lot more citizens.[15] In fact, Oakland, San Francisco County Marin County, and Santa Clara County all have pilot programs going that provide between $500 and $1,000 a month. The money right now is provided by private donations. These Bay area initiatives focus on "raising artists, mothers, or minorities out of poverty."[16]

Martin Luther King, Jr. pointed to the riots that took place during the 1960s and concluded that the solution to poverty is "to abolish it directly by a now widely discussed measure: the guaranteed income."†† The universal basic income would narrow the wealth gap and defuse a lot of anger fostered by unemployment.

## Funding a Universal Basic Income

Social scientists have proposed a number of possible ways to fund UBI. One method is to tax corporations that replace workers with robots, in effect a tax on robots. Bill Gates has argued that if a robot is going to do a human's job, it should also pay a person's income taxes.[17]

Another way of assuaging the impact of robots on unemployment and thus limit the amount of money required for a UBI would be to place quotas on different industries in terms of the percentage of jobs where robots could replace people. That idea sounds like the old Soviet Union's managed economy that failed miserably. An alternative is to raise taxes on income beyond a certain level, say a tax on income beyond $10 million dollars. Unfortunately, even if such a tax made its way past the barrier of lobbyists and senators financed by this very group, it is doubtful that there wouldn't be loopholes large enough to drive a truck through that would permit most people with those stratospheric incomes to avoid the tax.

Perhaps a way to justify paying for universal basic income that would soften opposition and persuade the wealthy that additional tax dollars are justified is to couple UBI with volunteer work in the community. Whether

---

†† See "Where Are We Going" in M.L. King, Jr. 2010. *Where Do We Go From Here: Chaos or Community?* (Beacon Press).

it's spending some hours volunteering in a daycare center or helping in other ways, the idea is that UBI would be giving people who receive the funds a sense of self-worth as well as improving their communities.[‡‡]

If UBI is not feasible, some analysts propose changing the nature of work in American culture so that 20 hours represents a full-time position. Such an approach would create more jobs, although it obviously would mean either an employer paying double for each human worker or the workers getting by on half a salary. Neither idea seems viable considering the economics as well as an American work culture of working more rather than fewer hours as a way of establishing a worker's value to a company.

Another alternative to the UBI would be a negative income tax. When a person's income is below a breakeven point, he or she would get a fraction of that difference as a payment from the government. The argument for this approach is that it would encourage people to work rather than live on a dole.[18]

## The Relationship Between Health Care and Employment

An unemployed man, clearly deranged, threatened in August 2021 to blow up the Library of Congress. His major complaint was that he lacked health insurance. Some social scientists suggest modifying the U.S. health care system by creating a public option and eliminating the link between employer and health insurance. Some point to Denmark as an example. In fact, Denmark also makes it easier for employers to fire employees but then provides these workers with enough income so that they can survive until they find another job.[§§]

The growing trend toward a *gig economy* where companies hire contract workers rather than workers with full benefits, including health care, creates another problem for social scientists to try to solve. While at least

---

[‡‡] See Chapter 10 in E. Brynjolfsson and A. McAfee. 2014. *The Second Machine Age: Work, Progress, and Prosperity in a Time of Brilliant Technology.*

[§§] "March of the Machines." June 25, 2016. economist.com. www.economist .com/leaders/2016/06/25/march-of-the-machines (accessed May 5, 2022).

one futurist lauds the gig economy as a *talent economy* and a wonderful situation for both employer and talented contract worker,[19] the truth is that the prospects of even more people in the future unemployed and uninsured is scary. A Brookings Institute study suggests that the government needs to consider creating flexible accounts that could be used for education, training, health insurance, life insurance, and retirement. It also suggests that companies that employ independent contractors should be charged 5 percent of these workers' earnings and the money used to support health subsidies.[¶¶]

In fact, there are a number of ideas circulating for providing a way to fund workers' health care and educational needs when they lose their jobs. Jerry Kaplan proposes what he calls a *job mortgage* that is secured by a worker's future earned income. When a worker loses his or her job, the mortgage payments would be suspended for a grace period until they find another job. He believes very much in the capitalist system, and rather than more government involvement, suggests that employers should be able to offer a potential employee a letter of intent indicating that it intends to hire that worker if he or she acquires certain skills, but that the letter would not be binding. Kaplan's idea decouples education from an individual employer and provides the free market version of an apprenticeship as the worker would use money from the job mortgage to pay for skill training.[20]

Jared Bernstein, a senior fellow at the Center on Budget and Policy Priorities, argues that if the private market is not providing enough jobs, then the government should engage in direct job creation. He points to a study by the Georgetown Center on Poverty and Inequality that examined 40 different programs over 40 years and found that most were successful when it came to things like improving workers' skills and ultimately reducing those workers' dependence on public benefits.[21]

## The Rebirth of Labor Unions

Labor unions developed out of the terrible abuse of workers at the turn of the 20th century. Corporations have been working with conservatives

---

[¶¶] See Chapter 5 in M. Muro, J. Whiton, and R. Maxim. 2019. *What Jobs Are Affected by AI.*

ever since to minimize labor's power and reach. During the past few decades, many companies moved to southern states where Right to Work laws resulted in less labor presence and lower salaries. In the future, it is possible that the sheer number of unemployed workers might kindle the rebirth of the labor movement, perhaps even a human labor union to combat the threat from robots. An MIT study criticizes U.S. labor policies as leftovers from an earlier time and pointed to the lack of protection for contract, temporary, and gig workers. It also pointed to the lack of portability of health insurance, medical family, and parental leave policies.[22]

## Government Retraining Programs

Automation will require the government to step up its programs to retrain workers, often those workers in mid-career. Most current federal programs are funded through the Workforce Innovation and Opportunity Act as well as the Trade Adjustment Assistance Program. An MIT automation study revealed that while close to 75 percent of participants found jobs, the earnings replacement ratios were in the 75 to 85 percent range depending on age.[23]

## Government Might Need Restructuring

The political pressure from large numbers of unemployed workers who blame automation and lack of government help for their situation might require a major restructuring of government to deal with this crisis. The glaring inequalities in wealth might force the passage of new anti-trust laws. They might also result in the elimination of the Electoral College and the passage of a universal voting law in order to ensure that the populace believes it has a major voice in how the government handles massive unemployment. Similarly, unrest could lead to campaign finance reform and even legislation to control social manipulation and the spread of disinformation.*** While these moves will strike many as very left wing and ultra-progressive in today's polarized political environment, tomorrow's

---

*** See Chapter 7 in "Is Politics Up to the Task?" in M, Muro, J. Whiton, and R. Maxim. 2019. *What Jobs Are Affected by AI?*

politicians viewing a situation that might be on the brink of chaos might make such moves politically expedient. As I indicated earlier in this chapter, this country has often swung back and forth between left of center and right of center decades. The right of center 1930s and its economic depression made Franklin D. Roosevelt's massive government programs politically feasible. Racial violence and civic unrest helped propel LBJ's Great Society programs of the 1960s. In any event, automation in the near future is bound to increase the pressure on politicians, educators, and social scientists as they grapple with ways to ensure that the quality of life does not fall dramatically as robots and artificial intelligence become key parts of everyday life.

# Glossary

**3D Printing**: A form of additive manufacturing where a printer repeatedly *prints* thin layers of material as it follows computer-assisted drawing instructions to print an entire three-dimensional object.

**4D Printing**: An enhanced form of 3D printing where material is used that can later change its form and function based on external stimuli.

**AI**: Artificial intelligence

**Artificial Intelligence**: A term used to describe when computers and machines mimic human behavior and simulate human intelligence.

**Amara's Law**: The theory that we overestimate the impact of technology in the short term and underestimate the effect in the long run.

**Augmented Reality**: A technology that augments reality. In other words, people might view a hotel and see information about that hotel displayed via special glasses.

**Big Data**: This term refers to truly massive datasets that can be characterized not only by their size, but also by the different types of data, the quality, and the value of that data.

**Bio Ink**: A substance usually composed of cells and a gel-like substance used to create a 3D scaffolding for printing human organs and tissue.

**Blockchain**: The blockchain consists of blocks of data on an ever-increasing number of distributed servers that communicate with each other in a peer-to-peer network with no single entity in control.

**Chatbot**: A software application used to conduct an online chat conversation via text or text-to-speech, in lieu of providing direct contact with a live human agent.

**Cobot**: A robot that is designed to work with people.

**CRISPR:** (Clustered Regularly Interspaced Short Palindromic Repeats), a very efficient method of editing genes.

**Cryptocurrency:** Digital money whose activity is tied to a blockchain.

**Data Analytics:** AI software that can analyze data and provide descriptive, predictive, and prescriptive information about that data.

**Deep Learning:** Using very large datasets to mimic the way humans think by creating what is known as a neural network.

**Fusion Energy:** Energy produced when the nuclei of small atoms stick together and fuse to release energy. This fusion creates electrically charged plasma that exists at temperatures higher than found on the Sun.

**Genomics:** The multidisciplinary field that focuses on genomes for various organisms, including humans as well on techniques for manipulating these genes.

**Green Technologies:** This phrase refers to technologies that contribute to sustaining or restoring the environment.

**Human Augmentation:** Enhancing human performance by appending some machine functionality.

**Internet of Things (IoT):** The term refers to the network of sensors attached to various objects that transmit their information via the Internet and, in turn, receive input and instructions back.

**Metaverse:** An immersive virtual world viewed as a successor to today's mobile Internet.

**Mixed Reality:** Technology that enables a person to view a real scene and *mix* in virtual reality. As an example, it is possible to view a room and then add a virtual piece of furniture to it to see if it fits in.

**Moore's Law**: Gordon Moore at Intel noticed in 1965 that the number of transistors in an electron circuit (essentially its processing power) appeared to double every year.

**Nanotechnology**: The manipulation molecules and atoms to create new materials in a scale of a billionth on a meter (nanometer).

**Narrow Artificial Intelligence**: AI that is limited to a specific task or set of tasks.

**Quantum Computing**: These computers utilize the equivalent of bits called qubits that can represent multiple degrees of ones and zeros states simultaneously and solve mathematical problems in minutes that might take years using conventional computers.

**Robot Process Automation (RPA)**: This type of automation describes software processes that never vary, so they don't require any real intelligence.

**Robot**: A programmable machine.

**Sexbot**: A robot with artificial intelligence designed to perform sex with humans.

**Smart Cities**: This phrase refers to cities that have widely deployed IoT networks.

**Smart Contract**: This means that software can be added to the blockchain that creates a series of conditions that must be met for certain actions to take place as part of a contract.

**Soft Skills**: Skills that humans possess that give them an advantage over robots. These skills generally include empathy, critical thinking, adaptability, communication, creativity, sociability, curiosity, problem-solving, persuasiveness, flexibility, and conscientiousness.

**Supervised Learning**: AI pros provide a correct dataset and a test dataset along with a set of rules or parameters. They then *teach* the machine by having it answer and then correct it when it makes the wrong choice.

**Universal Basic Income (UBI)**: A government-established basic living stipend paid to all citizens.

**Unsupervised Learning**: Unsupervised learning in artificial intelligence consists of providing a labeled dataset and letting the machine come up with its own criteria rather than establishing parameters.

**Virtual Reality**: This term refers to a technology that totally immerses someone in a simulated reality.

# Notes

## Foreword

1. Diamandis and Kotler (2020), p. 23.

## Chapter 1

1. Johnson (n.d.).
2. Byrnes (2017).
3. BER Staff (2020).
4. Manyika, Lund, Chui, Bughin, Woetzel, Batra, Ko, and Sanghvi (2017).
5. Wyatt and Hecker (2006).
6. Le Clair (2019), p. 7.
7. Roose (2019).
8. Kellnar (2017).
9. Oppenheimer (2019).
10. Perelmuter (2021), p. 281.
11. Eitel-Porter (2018), p. 39.

## Chapter 2

1. Eitel-Porter (2018), p. 28.
2. Diamandis and Kotler (2020), pp. 94–105.
3. Eitel-Porter (2018), pp. 12–13.
4. Kelly (2014).
5. National Science Technology Council Committee on Technology (NSTC) (2016), p. 16.
6. Autor, Mindell, and Reynolds (2020), p. 40.
7. Swanson (2015).
8. Lin (2020).

9. Moore (2014).

10. Kellnar (2017).

11. World Economic Forum (2020), p. 28.

12. Harris, Kimson, and Schwedel (2018), p. 23.

13. Diorio (2020).

14. Linn (2018).

15. Schroer (2022a).

16. Markoff (2011).

17. Faggella (2021).

18. Marr (2020).

19. Schroer (2022a).

20. Thomas and Nordii (2022a).

21. Schroer (2022a).

22. Maguire (2019).

23. Diamandis and Kotler (2020), p. 105.

24. O'Connor (2018).

25. Harris, Kimson, and Schwedel (2018), p. 26.

26. Autor, Mindell, and Reynolds (2020), p. 44.

27. Stahl (2021).

28. Harris, Kimson, and Schwedel (2018), p. 27.

29. Lin (2020).

30. Venkat (2020).

31. Columbus (2020).

32. Smith and Anderson (2014).

33. Najibi (2020).

34. Stone, Brooks, Brynjolfsson, Calo, Etzioni, Hager, Hirschberg, Kalyanakrishnan, Kamar, Kraus, Leyton-Brown, Parkes, Press, Saenian, Shah, Tambe, and Teller (2016), p. 11.

35. Micron (n.d.).

36. Ibid.

37. Gregg, Duncan, and Siddiqui (2021).

38. Stone, Brooks, Brynjolfsson, Calo, Etzioni, Hager, Hirschberg, Kalyanakrishnan, Kamar, Kraus, Leyton-Brown, Parkes, Press, Saenian, Shah, Tambe, and Teller (2016), p. 41.

39. Simonite (2021).

40. Lin (2020).

41. Wooldridge (2020), p. 156.
42. Marshall (2021).
43. MacRumors Staff (2022).
44. Bertoncello, Martens, Möller, and Schneiderbauer (2021).
45. Ng (2022).
46. Autor, Mindell, and Reynolds (2020), p. 40.

## Chapter 3

1. Autor, Mindell, and Reynolds (2020), p. 46.
2. RBR Staff (2020).
3. Sharma (2019).
4. Knight (2022).
5. Maishman (2022).
6. Thomas (2022a).
7. Hao (2021).
8. Harris, Kimson, and Schwedel (2018), p. 31.
9. ABI Research (2019).
10. Moutafis (2021).
11. Acemoglu and Restrepo (2019).
12. Lin, Abney, and Bekey (2012), p. 224.
13. Templeton (2021).
14. Thomas (2022a).
15. Autor, Mindell, and Reynolds (2020), p. 40.
16. Ibid, p. 47.
17. Guillot (2019).
18. Hao (2021).
19. Matthews (2020).
20. Weinberg (2019).
21. Su (2020).
22. O'Brien (2020).
23. Acemoglu and Restrepo (2019).
24. Harwell (2019).
25. Matthews (2020).
26. Simon (2021).
27. RTN Staff (2019).

28. Hymowitz (2017).

29. Shaw (2019).

30. Schroer (2022b).

31. Bomey (2017).

32. Thomas (2022).

33. Stone, Brooks, Brynjolfsson, Calo, Etzioni, Hager, Hirschberg, Kalyanakrishnan, Kamar, Kraus, Leyton-Brown, Parkes, Press, Saenian, Shah, Tambe, and Teller (2016), p. 68.

34. Daley (2022).

35. Sturgeon (2017).

36. McFarland (2017).

37. Yamazaki, Nishio, Ishiguro, Nørskov, Ishiguro, and Balistreri (2014).

38. Simon (2017).

39. Simon (2018).

40. Petrovic (2020).

41. Petrovic (2021).

42. Baral (2017).

43. Allday (2011).

44. Etzioni and Etzioni (2017).

45. Armstrong (2013).

46. Yonck (2017), pp. 81–82.

47. Kolhatkar (2017).

## Chapter 4

1. Dybuncio (2012).

2. Carolo (2021).

3. Piewa (2019).

4. Ibid.

5. Ellis (2020).

6. Tong (2020).

7. Manyika, Lund, Chui, Bughin, Woetzel, Batra, Ko, and Sanghvi (2017).

8. "3D Printing Clothes at Home Could Be a Reality by 2050" (2013).

# Chapter 5

1. Lau (2021).
2. McLellan (2019), p. 6.

# Chapter 6

1. Kolmer (2022).
2. Tangermann (2021).
3. Pickerel (2021).
4. Frangoul (2021b).
5. Frangoul (2021a).
6. Winkler (2021).
7. Roberts (2020).
8. Kuadii (2021).
9. Schreiber (2021).
10. Ibid.
11. Hummel, Lesne, and Radlinger, Golbaz, Langan, Takahashi, Mulholland, Stott, Haire, Mittermaier, and Gaudois (2017).
12. Tomer, Kane, and George (2021).
13. Jung (2021).
14. Hennick (2017).
15. Winston and Lovins (2021).
16. Schindelheim (2022).
17. Kolmer (2022).
18. Gerencer (2021).
19. Kurtuy (2022).
20. Fernandez (2021).
21. Schatt and Lobl (2011).

# Chapter 7

1. Berger-de Leon, Reinbacher, and Wee (2018).
2. Petrov (2022).
3. Ibid.

4. Thomas (2022b).

5. Meola (2021).

6. Wolf (2021).

7. Robb (2022).

8. Petrov (2022b).

# Chapter 8

1. Purdy (2022).

2. Robertson (2022a).

3. Robertson (2022b).

4. Christensen and Robinson (2022).

5. Elmasry, Hazan, Khan, Kelly, Srivastava, Yee, and Zemmel (2022), p. 20.

6. Karpf (2021).

7. Lin (2022).

8. ASU News Service (2020).

9. Thomas (2021a).

10. Raftery (2022).

11. ASU News Service (2020).

12. Knight (2019).

13. Tayeb (2021).

14. Demaitre (2018).

15. Girdhar (2020).

16. Lin (2022).

# Chapter 9

1. Marr (2020), p. 3.

2. Vuleta (2021).

3. Tudor (2020).

4. Ross (2016), p. 153.

5. McDonald (2013).

6. Indeed Editorial Team (2021).

7. Durcevic (2020).

8. Petrov (2022).

9. Stedman (2022).
10. Morgan (2021).
11. Miller (2020).
12. White (2022).

## Chapter 10

1. Zimmer (2021).
2. Prabhune (2021).
3. Ruby and Singh (2017).
4. Ibid.
5. Neufeld (2021).
6. Fortune Business Insights (2022).
7. Robitzski (2020).
8. Barfield and Williams (2021), p. 11.
9. Tangermann (2019).
10. Barfield and Williams (2021), p. 11.

## Chapter 11

1. Drexler (2013), p. 24.
2. Perelmuter (2021), p. 184.
3. Sahoo (2020).
4. Marr (2020), p. 276.
5. Sahoo (2020).
6. Rahman (2020).

## Chapter 12

1. Lichfield (2020), p. 41.
2. Fuge (2021).
3. Lee (2021).
4. Dormehl (2018).
5. Werner (2021).
6. Williams (2021).
7. Ibid.

8. Martin (2021).
9. Fountain (2020).

## Chapter 13

1. DeRocco (2022).
2. 24/7 Staff (2018).
3. Bughin, Hazan, Lund, Dahlstrom, Wiesinger, and Subramaniam (2018).
4. Heffernan (n.d.).
5. Heckman and Kautz (2012).
6. Gardner (1983).
7. Goldman (1995).
8. Bradberry and Greaves (2009).

## Chapter 14

1. Smith and Anderson (2017).
2. Aoun (2017).
3. Brynjolfsson and McAfee (2014), pp. 196–197.
4. Stone, Brooks, Brynjolfsson, Calo, Etzioni, Hager, Hirschberg, Kalyanakrishnan, Kamar, Kraus, Leyton-Brown, Parkes, Press, Saenian, Shah, Tambe, and Teller (2016), p. 18.
5. Miller (2017).
6. Bomey (2017).
7. Autor, Mindell, and Reynolds (2020), p. 94.
8. Ibid, p. 82.
9. Shell (2018).
10. Muro, Whiton, and Maxim (2019).
11. Moutafis (2021).
12. Benson (2020).
13. Singh (2020).
14. Miller (2017).
15. Cowan (2020).
16. Bedain (2021).
17. Dill (2017).

18. Stone, Brooks, Brynjolfsson, Calo, Etzioni, Hager, Hirschberg, Kalyanakrishnan, Kamar, Kraus, Leyton-Brown, Parkes, Press, Saenian, Shah, Tambe, and Teller (2016), p. 18.

19. Le Clair (2019), pp. 81–89.

20. Kaplan (2015), p. 13.

21. Miller (2017).

22. Autor, Mindell, and Reynolds (2020), p. 34.

23. Ibid, p. 97.

# Bibliography

"10 Best Global machine Learning Certifications & Training in April, 2022. n.d. Favouriteblog.com.

"12 Jobs That Robots and AI Will Replace in the Future and 12 That Won't." October 5, 2021. savion.com.

"21 Jobs of the Future, A Guide to Getting and Staying Employed Over the Next 10 Years." November 2017. *Cognizant Center for the Future of Work*.

"300+ Internet of Things Courses 2022 Learn Online for Free." n.d. classcentral .com

"3D Printing Clothes at Home Could Be a Reality by 2050." March 2013. Innovationtorronto.com. https://innovationtoronto.com/2013/03/3d-printing-clothes-at-home-could-be-a-reality-by-2050/ (accessed April 26, 2022).

"Applications of Nanotechnology." n.d. www.nano.gov.

"Artificial Intelligence and Robotics: From a Labour and Tax perspective." May 2018. cms.com.

"Artificial Intelligence Creates More Jobs." 2018. *Beyond Limits News*.

"Brain-Computer Interface Lets Three People Play Video Games Using Their Minds." July 2, 2019. Technologynetworks.com.

"Examples of Successful Virtual Reality Marketing." January 19, 2018. *Digital Marketing Institute.com*.

"Fastest Growing Occupations." April 19, 2022. *U.S. Bureau of Labor Statistics*.

"Half Man, Half Circuit: Who Are the People Who Are Choosing to Become Cyborgs?" March 24, 2016. Open.edu.

"Healthcare Is Only the Beginning: 15 Big Industries CRISPR Technology Could Disrupt." August 1, 2018. cbinsights.com.

"How Remote Work Has Accelerated Automation." February 26, 2021. *Fisherstech*.

"Is Cryptocurrency the Future of Online Gaming?" April 19, 2022. *The Daily Gazette*.

"Nanotechnology Market by Type (Nanosensor and Nanodevice) and Application (Electronics, Energy, Chemical Manufacturing, Aerospace & Defense, Healthcare, and Others) Global Opportunity Analysis and Industry Forecast: 2021-2030." July 2021. Alliedmarketresearch.com.

"Nanotechnology Market, By Type (Nanosensors, Nanodevice, Nanomaterials, Others), By Application (Information Technology (IT), Homeland Security, Medicine, Transportation, Food Safety, Others), By End-use, and By Region Forecast to 2030." February 2022. Emergenresearch.com.

"The 36th Annual Space Symposium Special Edition." 2021. swfound.org.

"The Future of Blockchain Technology in 2022." January 7, 2022. www
.getsmarter.com.

"The Quantum Decade." June 10, 2021. IBM.com.

"What Happened When a Chinese TV Station Replaced Its Meteorologist With
a Chatbot." January 12, 2016. *Washington Post.*

"What Is Big Data Analytics and Why Is It So Important?" April 3, 2022.
Simplilearn.com.

24/7 Staff. January 25, 2018. "Are Robots Going to Replace Workers in the
Warehouse?" supplychain247.com. www.supplychain247.com/article/are_robots
_going_to_replace_people_in_the_warehouse (accessed May 18, 2022).

ABI Research. March 26, 2019. "50,000 Warehouses to Use Robots by 2025 as
Barriers to Entry Fall and AI Innovation Accelerates." Press Release. www
.abiresearch.com/press/50000-warehouses-use-robots-2025-barriers-entry-
fall-and-ai-innovation-accelerates/ (accessed May 5, 2022).

Acemoglu, D. and J. Robinson. 2012. *Why Nations Fail: The Origins of Power,
Prosperity, and Poverty.* Random House Digital, Inc.

Acemoglu, D. and P. Restrepo. June 2020. "Robots and Jobs: Evidence From US
Labor Markets." *Journal of Political Economy* 128, no. 6.

Acemoglu, D. and P. Restrepo. Spring 2019. "Automation and New Tasks:
How Technology Displaces and Reinstates Labor." *Journal of Economic
Perspectives* 33, no. 2, pp. 3–30. www.aeaweb.org/articles?id=10.1257/
jep.33.2.3 (accessed May 22, 2022).

Aggarwal, A. January 20, 2018. "Domains in Which Artificial Intelligence Is
Rivaling Humans." scryanalytics.com.

Allday, E. May 30, 2011. "UCSF Pharmacy Lets Robots Prepare the Meds." *SF
Gate.* www.sfgate.com/news/article/UCSF-pharmacy-lets-robots-prepare-
the-meds-2369880.php (accessed April 25, 2022).

Anderson, B.C. n.d. "In prospect: The Shape of Work to Come 2017." Manhattan
Institute for Policy Research.

Aoun, J.E. 2017. *Robot-Proof: Higher Education in the Age of Artificial Intelligence.*
MIT Press.

Armstrong, D. September 17, 2013. "Emotional Attachment to Robots Could
Affect Outcome on Battlefield." *UW News.* University of Washington. www
.washington.edu/news/2013/09/17/emotional-attachment-to-robots-could-
affect-outcome-on-battlefield/ (accessed April 25, 2022).

ASU News Service. December 22, 2020. "Exploring New Worlds in Virtual
Reality." news.asu.edu. https://news.asu.edu/20201222-creativity-exploring-
new-worlds-virtual-reality (accessed April 28, 2022).

Atkinson, R. n.d. www.csmonitor.com/Technology/Breakthroughs-Voices/2017/
0510/Think-technology-is-disrupting-the-job-market-like-never-before-Think-again.

Autor, D., D.A. Mindell, and E. Reynolds. 2020. *The Work of the Future: Building Better Jobs in an Age of Machines*, pp. 34–97. MIT. https://workofthefuture.mit.eduhttps://workofthefuture.mit.edu (accessed May 21, 2022).

Autor, D., A. Salomons, and B. Seegmiller. July 2021. "New Frontiers: The Origins and Content of New Work, 1940–2018." blueprintlabs.mit.edu.

Ball, P. November 17, 2021. "The Chase for Fusion Energy." nature.com.

Barfield, W. and A. Williams. 2021. "Cyborgs and Enhancement Technology." In W. Barfield, and S. Blodgett-Ford, ed., *Human Enhancement Technologies and Our Merger with Machines*, pp. 5–23. Basel: MDPI.

Baral, S. April 24, 2017. "5 Robots That Are About to Revolutionize the Workforce—and Put Jobs at Risk." mic.com. www.mic.com/articles/174936/5-robots-that-are-about-to-revolutionize-the-workforce-and-put-jobs-at-risk (accessed April 25, 2022).

Bedain, J. July 21, 2021. "Universal Basic Income? California Moves to Be First State to Fund Pilot Efforts." kpbs.org. www.kpbs.org/news/economy/2021/07/20/universal-basic-income-california-moves-be-first-s (accessed May 5, 2022).

Benson, A. December 6, 2020. "Here Are the Average Retirement Savings by Age: Is It Enough?" marketwatch.com. www.marketwatch.com/story/here-are-the-average-retirement-savings-by-age-is-it-enough-2020-11-16 (accessed May 5, 2022).

BER Staff. April 2, 2020. "The Future of Employment in the Age of Robots and AI." Berkeley Economic Review. https://econreview.berkeley.edu/the-future-of-employment-in-the-age-of-robots-and-ai/ (accessed June 25, 2022).

Berger-de Leon, M., T. Reinbacher, and D. Wee. March 21, 2018. "The IOT as a Growth Driver." Mckinsey.com. www.mckinsey.com/business-functions/mckinsey-digital/our-insights/the-iot-as-a-growth-driver (accessed April 28, 2022).

Bertoncello, M., C. Martens, T. Möller, and T. Schneiderbauer. February 11, 2021. "Unlocking the Full Life-Cycle Value From Connected-Car Data." Mckinsey.com. www.mckinsey.com/industries/automotive-and-assembly/our-insights/unlocking-the-full-life-cycle-value-from-connected-car-data (accessed August 2, 2022).

Birch, D.G.W. 1987. *Job Creation in America: How Our Smallest Companies Put the Most People to Work*. Free Press.

Bomey, N. February 6, 2017. "Automation Puts Jobs in Peril." *USA Today*. www.usatoday.com/story/money/2017/02/06/special-report-automation-puts-jobs-peril/96464788/ (accessed April 25, 2022).

Bradberry, T.D. and J. Greaves. 2009. *Emotional Intelligence 2.0*. TalentSmith.

Brady, B. and C. Mendez. April 26, 2022. "100+ Robotics Online Classes You Can Take for Free."classcentral.com.

Brynjolfsson, E. and A. McAfee. 2014. *The Second Machine Age: Work, Progress, and Prosperity in a Time of Brilliant Technology,* pp. 196–197. Norton.

Bughin, J., E. Hazan, S. Lund, P. Dahlström, A. Wiesinger, and A. Subramaniam. May 23, 2018. "Skill Shift: Automation and the Future of the Workforce." mckinsey.com. www.mckinsey.com/featured-insights/future-of-work/skill-shift-automation-and-the-future-of-the-workforce (accessed May 18, 2022).

Byrnes, N. February 7, 2017. "As Goldman Embraces Automation, Even the Masters of the Universe Are Threatened." technologyreview.com. www.technologyreview.com/2017/02/07/154141/as-goldman-embraces-automation-even-the-masters-of-the-universe-are-threatened/ (accessed April 30, 2022).

Carolo, L. January 13, 2021. "3D Printed Organs/Body Parts: Most Promising Projects." All3DP.com. https://all3dp.com/2/most-promising-3d-printed-organs-for-transplant/ (accessed April 26, 2022).

Christensen, L. and A. Robinson. 2022. *The Potential Global Economic Impact of the Metaverse.* AG Analysis Group. www.analysisgroup.com/globalassets/insights/publishing/2022-the-potential-global-economic-impact-of-the-metaverse.pdf (accessed August 5, 2022).

Colagrossi, M. May 28, 2018. "What's the Difference Between A.I., Machine Learning, and Robotics?" bigthink.com.

Colin, N. and B. Palier. July/August 2015. "Social Policy for a Digital Age." *Foreign Affairs* 94, no. 4, pp. 29–33.

Columbus, L. May 18, 2020. "10 Ways AI Is Improving Manufacturing in 2020." *Forbes.* www.forbes.com/sites/louiscolumbus/2020/05/18/10-ways-ai-is-improving-manufacturing-in-2020/?sh=2146911e1e85 (accessed May 21, 2022).

Cookson, C. and P. McGee. July 19, 2019. "Cyborgs: Elon Musk and the New Era of Neuroscience." ft.com.

Cowan, J. July 1, 2020. "Should Californians Get Guaranteed Income?" nytimes.com. www.nytimes.com/2020/07/01/us/ubi-california.html (accessed May 5, 2022).

Cunniffe, A. August 30, 2017. "Don't Fear Automation Technology—Embrace It." *GE News.*

Daley, S. April 23, 2022. "10 Publicly Traded Companies That Are Betting on Robotics." *Built In.* https://builtin.com/robotics/publicly-traded-robotics-companies (accessed April 25, 2022).

Daley, S. May 28, 2021. "23 Examples of Artificial Intelligence Shaking Up Business as Usual." *Built In.*

Demaitre, E. October 14, 2018. "AR, VR Are Transforming the Nature of Work Says PTC on Manufacturing Day." roboticsbusinessreview.com. www.roboticsbusinessreview.com/ar-vr-manufacturing-day-ptc/ (accessed April 28, 2022).

DeRocco, L. February 18, 2022. "Our Cobot Co-Workers." automation.com. www.automation.com/en-us/articles/february-2022/our-cobot-co-workers (accessed May 15, 2022).

Diamandis, P.H. and S. Kotler. 2020. *The Future Is Faster Than You Think: How Converging Technologies Are Transforming Business, Industries, and Our Lives*, pp. 94–181. Simon and Schuster.

Dill, K. February 17, 2017. "Bill Gates: Job-Stealing Robots Should Pay Income Taxes." cnbc.com. www.cnbc.com/2017/02/17/bill-gates-job-stealing-robots-should-pay-income-taxes.html (accessed May 5, 2022).

Diorio, S. May 8, 2020. "Realizing the Growth Potential for AI." forbes.com. www.forbes.com/sites/forbesinsights/2020/05/08/realizing-the-growth-potential-of-ai/?sh=2ff2607233f3 (accessed April 25, 2020).

Dizkes, P. May 4, 2020. "How Many Jobs Do Robots Really Replace?" *TechXplore*.

Dormehl, L. April 22, 2018. "Want a Future-Proof Degree? Head to Colorado for Asteroid Mining." digitaltrends.com. www.digitaltrends.com/space/colorado-school-of-mines-space-resources-mining/ (accessed May 18, 2022).

Dozier, R. June 3, 2019. "This Clothing Line Was Designed by AI." *Vice*.

Drexler, K. 2013. *Radical Abundance: How a Revolution in Nanotechnology Will Change Civilization*, p. 24. PublicAffairs.

Durcevic, S. October 21, 2020. "18 Examples of Data Analytics in Healthcare That Can Save People." Datapine.com. www.datapine.com/blog/datapine.com/blog/big-data-examples-in-healthcare/ (accessed May 2, 2022).

Dybuncio, M. February 6, 2012. "Woman Gets World's First 3D Printed Jaw Transplant." *CBS News*. www.cbsnews.com/news/woman-gets-worlds-first-3d-printed-jaw-transplant/ (accessed April 26, 2022).

Eitel-Porter, R. 2018. *AI Explained: A Guide For Executives*, pp. 12–39. Accenture. www.accenture.com/us-en/insights/artificial-intelligence/artificial-intelligence-explained-executives (accessed April 24, 2022).

Ellis, G. August 4, 2020. "3D Printing in Construction: Growth, Benefits, and Challenges." *Digital Builder*. https://constructionblog.autodesk.com/3d-printing-construction/ (accessed April 26, 2022).

Elmasry, T., E. Hazan, H. Khan, G. Kelly, L. Yee, S. Srivastava, and R.W. Zemmel. 2022. *Value Creation in the Metaverse: The Real Business of the Virtual World*, p. 20. McKinsey.com. www.mckinsey.com/~/media/mckinsey/business%20functions/marketing%20and%20sales/our%20insights/value%20creation%20in%20the%20metaverse/Value-creation-in-the-metaverse.pdf (accessed August 5, 2022).

Etzioni, A. and O. Etzioni. May–June 2017. "Pros and Cons of Autonomous Weapons Systems." *Military Review*. www.armyupress.army.mil/Journals/Military-Review/English-Edition-Archives/May-June-2017/Pros-and-Cons-of-Autonomous-Weapons-Systems/ (accessed April 25, 2022).

Faggella, D. September 7, 2021. "AI in Law and Legal Practice—A Comprehensive View of 35 Current Applications." Emerj.com. https://emerj.com/ai-sector-overviews/ai-in-law-legal-practice-current-applications/ (accessed April 25, 2022).

Fernandez, L.N. September 4, 2021. "Reskilling Workers for the Green Economy." www.xprize.org. www.xprize.org/prizes/rapidskilling/articles/reskilling-workers-for-the-green-economy.

Ford, M. 2015. *Rise of the Robots: Technology and the Threat of a Jobless Future.* Basic Books.

Fortune Business Insights. January 2022. "Pharmaceutics/Genomics Market." fortunebusinessinsights.com. www.fortunebusinessinsights.com/industry-reports/genomics-market-100941 (accessed May 2, 2022).

Fountain, H. September 29, 2020. "Compact Fusion Reactor Is 'Very Likely to Work, Studies Suggest." nytimes.com. www.nytimes.com/2020/09/29/climate/nuclear-fusion-reactor.html (accessed May 19, 2022).

Frangoul, A. March 30, 2021a. "U.S. Announces Plans to Ramp Up Offshore Wind Capacity in a Big Way." *CNBC.* www.cnbc.com/2021/03/30/the-us-announces-plans-to-ramp-up-offshore-wind-capacity-in-a-big-way.html (accessed April 28, 2022).

Frangoul, A. April 30, 2021b. "Wind Energy Could Generate 3.3 Million Jobs Within Five Years, Industry Body Claims." *CNBC.* www.cnbc.com/2021/04/30/wind-energy-could-generate-3point3-million-jobs-in-next-five-years-gwec.html (accessed April 25, 2022).

Frank, M., P. Roehrig, and B. Pring. 2017. *What to Do When Machines Do Everything: How to Get Ahead in a World of AI, Algorithms, Bots, and Big Data.* Wiley.

Frey, C.B. and M.A. Osborne. January 1, 2017. "The Future of Employment: How susceptible Are Jobs to Computerisation?" *Technological Forecasting and Social Change* 114, pp. 254–280.

Frey, C.B. and M.A. Osborne. September 17, 2013. "The Future of Employment: How susceptible Are Jobs to Computerisation?" *Oxford Martin Programme on Technology and Employment.*

Fuge, L. July 2021. "China Demonstrates Most Powerful Quantum Computer." cosmosmagazine.com. https://cosmosmagazine.com/science/china-demonstrates-most-powerful-quantum-computer/ (accessed May 17, 2022).

Gardner, H. 1983. *Frames of Mind: The Theory of Multiple Intelligences.* Basic Books.

Gerencer, T. November 17, 2021. "Green Careers—150+ Sustainability Careers and How to Get Them Fast." https://zety.com/blog/sustainability-careers.

Girdhar, A. November 27, 2020. "The Limitations of Virtual Reality." appypie.com. www.appypie.com/virtual-reality-limitations (accessed April 28, 2022).

Goldin, C. and L.F. Katz. 1998. "The Origins of Technology-Skill Complementarity." *The Quarterly Journal of Economics* 113, no. 3, pp. 693–732.

Goldman, D. 1995. *Emotional Intelligence*. Random House.

Goos, M. and A. Manning. 2007. "Lousy and Lovely Jobs: The Rising Polarization of Work in Britain." *The Review of Economics and Statistics* 89, no. 1, pp. 118–133.

Gregg, A., I. Duncan, and F. Siddiqui. August 16, 2021. "Tesla Autopilot Faces U.S. Safety Regulator's Scrutiny." *Washington Post*. www.washingtonpost.com/business/2021/08/16/tesla-autopilot-investigation-nhtsa/n (accessed April 25, 2022).

Guillot, C. July 8, 2019. "Beyond Big-Name Uses, Robots Are Becoming More Prevalent in Retail." *STORES: NRF's MAGAZINE*. https://nrf.com/blog/retails-robot-revolution (accessed April 25, 2022).

Halsey, A. December 18, 2019. "The Big Challenges of 3D Printing." *Manufacturing Tomorrow*.

Hanna, K.T. March 25, 2021. "The Top 20 Programs for Studying Artificial Intelligence." TechTarget.com.

Hao, K. August 6, 2021. "A New Generation of AI-Powered Robots Is Taking Over Warehouses." *MIT Technology Review*. www.technologyreview.com/2021/08/06/1030802/ai-robots-take-over-warehouses/ (accessed April 25, 2022).

Harris, K., A. Kimson, and A. Schwedel. February 7, 2018. "Labor 2030: The Collision of Demographics, Automation and Inequality." *The Business Environment of the 2020s Will Be More Volatile and Economic Swings More Extreme*, pp. 23–31. Bain and Company. www.bain.com/insights/labor-2030-the-collision-of-demographics-automation-and-inequality/ (accessed May 21, 2022).

Harwell, D. June 6, 2019. "As Walmart Turns to Robots, It's the Human Workers Who Feel Like Machines." *Washington Post*. www.washingtonpost.com/technology/2019/06/06/walmart-turns-robots-its-human-workers-who-feel-like-machines/ (accessed April 25, 2022).

Heckman, J.J. and T.D. Kautz. June 2012. "Hard Evidence on Soft Skills." National Bureau of Economic Research. www.nber.org/papers/w18121 (accessed May 18, 2022).

Heffernan, M. n.d. "The Workplace Skills That Survive the AI Revolution." learnosity.com. https://learnosity.com/edtech-blog/workplace-skills-that-will-survive-the-ai-revolution/ (accessed My 18, 2022).

Hennick, C. September 25, 2017. "Retraining American Workers for Green Energy Jobs." USGBC.org. www.thecgo.org/benchmark/retraining-for-green-initiatives/ (accessed April 26, 2022).

Hinds, R. April 2018. "By 2020, "You're More Likely to Have a Conversation With This Than With Your Spouse: Our Communication Patterns Are Changing. Here's What You Need to Know." *Inc*.

Hummel, P., D. Lesne, J. Radinger, C. Golbaz, C. Langan, K. Takahashi, D. Mulholland, A. Stott, G. Haire, M. Mittermaier, and N. Gaudois. May 18, 2017. "UBS Evidence Lab Electric Car Teardown—Disruption Ahead?" Ubs.com. https://neo.ubs.com/shared/d1wkuDlEbYPjF/ (accessed April 26, 2022).

Hymowitz, K.S. 2017. "The Mother of All Disruptions." *City Journal Magazine.* www.city-journal.org/html/mother-all-disruptions-15251.html (accessed April 25, 2022).

Idzikowski, L., ed. 2020. *AI, Robots, and the Future of the Human Race.* Greenhaven Publishing.

Indeed Editorial Team. April 2, 2021. "8 Careers in Robotics to Consider." Indeed.com.

Indeed Editorial Team. June 17, 2021. "9 Ways Industries Use Big Data." Indeed .com. www.indeed.com/career-advice/career-development/using-big-data (accessed May 2, 2022).

International Federation of Robotics. March 26, 2019. *Press Release.*

Ishmael, K.E. August 6, 2020. "Qualcomm Institute-Based Startup Receives Funding to Continue Development of Opioid Sensor." *UC San Diego Center News.*

Isidore, C. February 6, 2018. "Machines Are Driving Wall Street's Wild Ride, Not Humans." *CNN.*

Jamie, D. June 13, 2019. "TOP 10 3D Printing & Additive Manufacturing University Degrees." 3Dnatives.com.

Jennings, K. February 16, 2011. "My Puny Human Brain." *Slate.*

Johnson, B. n.d. "The Great Horse Manure Crisis of 1894." HistoricUK.Com. www.historic-uk.com/HistoryUK/HistoryofBritain/Great-Horse-Manure-Crisis-of-1894/ (accessed April 4, 2022).

Jung, D. November 17, 2021. "Retraining for Green Initiatives." *The Center for Growth Opportunity at Utah state University.* www.thecgo.org/benchmark/ retraining-for-green-initiatives/ (accessed April 25, 2022).

Kaplan, J. 2015. *Humans Need Not Apply: A guide to Wealth and Work in the Age of Artificial Intelligence*, p. 13. Yale University Press.

Karpf, D. July 27, 2021. "Virtual Reality Is the White Rich Kid of Technology." *Wired Magazine.* www.wired.com/story/virtual-reality-rich-white-kid-of-technology/ (accessed April 28, 2022).

Kasparov, G. February 11, 2010. "The Chess Master and the Computer." *New York Review of Books.*

Kellnar, D. December 12, 2017. "The State of AI 2017: What Matters Most." medium.com. https://medium.com/mmc-writes/the-state-of-ai-2017-what-matters-most-1c87d8d4e81c (accessed April 25, 2022).

Kelly, K. October 27, 2014. "The Three Breakthroughs That Have Finally Unleashed AI on the World." *Wired Magazine.* www.wired.com/2014/10/future-of-artificial-intelligence/ (accessed April 25, 2022).

Kleeman, J. April 27, 2017. "The Race to Build the World's First Sex Robot." *The Guardian.*

Klemens, S. April 1, 2022. "Fintech Boot Camps: A Complete Guide." TechGuide.org.

Knight, W. August 9, 2019. "You Can Now Practice Firing Someone in Virtual Reality." Technologyreview.com. www.technologyreview.com/2019/08/09/133799/you-can-now-practice-firing-someone-in-virtual-reality/ (accessed April 18, 2022).

Knight, W. March 14, 2020. "AI Is Coming for Your Most Mind-Numbing Office Tasks." Wired.com.

Knight, W. June 28, 2022. "This Warehouse Robot Reads Human Body Language." Wired.com. www.wired.com/story/warehouse-robot-reads-body-language/.

Kolhatkar, S. October 23, 2017. "Welcoming Our New Robot Overlords." *The New Yorker.* www.newyorker.com/magazine/2017/10/23/welcoming-our-new-robot-overlords (accessed April 25, 2022).

Kolmer, C. April 24, 2022. "18 Inspiring Renewable Energy Job Creation Statistics [2022]." *Zippia.* www.zippia.com/advice/renewable-energy-job-creation-statistics/ (accessed April 28, 2022).

Kopestinsky, A. April 29, 2021. "25 Astonishing Self-Driving Car Statistics for 2021." PolicyAdvice.net.

Kuadii, J. October 29, 2021. "19 Fascinating Green Building Statistics." Seed Scientific. https://seedscientific.com/green-building-statistics/ (accessed April 28, 2022).

Kurtuy, A. April 29, 2020. "2021 Guide to Green Careers—All You Need to Know." Novoresume.com. https://novoresume.com/career-blog/green-careers.

Lau, Y. November 8, 2021. "Cryptocurrencies Hit Market Cap of $3 Trillion for the First Time as Bitcoin and Ether Reach Record Highs." *Fortune.* https://fortune.com/2021/11/09/cryptocurrency-market-cap-3-trillion-bitcion-ether-shiba-inu/ (accessed April 26, 2022).

Le Clair, C. 2019. *Invisible Robots in the Quiet of the Night: How AI and Automation Will Restructure the Workforce,* pp. 7–89. Forrester.

Lee, C. March 8, 2021. "Programmable Optical Quantum Computer Arrives Late, Steals the Show." arstechnica.com. https://arstechnica.com/science/2021/03/programmable-optical-quantum-computer-arrives-late-steals-the-show/ (accessed May 17, 2022).

Lichfield, G. March–April 2020. "To Reign Supreme: What the Race to Build a Quantum Computer Reveals About Google and IBM." *MIT Technology Review*, no. 38–45, p. 41.

Lin, P., K. Abney, and G.A. Bekey. 2012. *Robot Ethics: The Ethical and Social Implications of Robotics*, p. 224. MIT Press.

Lin, Y. August 22, 2020. "Artificial Intelligence Statistics You Need to Know in 2021." *Oberlo*. www.oberlo.com/blog/artificial-intelligence-statistics (accessed April 25, 2022).

Lin, Y. February 12, 2022. "10 Virtual Reality Statistics Every Marketer Should Know in 2022 [Infographic]." Oberlo.com. www.oberlo.com/blog/virtual-reality-statistics (accessed April 28, 2022).

Linn, N.O. April 7, 2018. "XiaoIce: When a chatbot Chat Moves Up to Human-Sounding Flow." TechXplore.com. https://techxplore.com/news/2018-04-xiaoice-chatbot-chat-human-sounding.html (accessed June 27, 2022).

Lonsdale, J. April 12, 2017. "AI and Robots Will Take Our Jobs—But Better Ones Will Emerge for Us." *Wired Magazine*.

Lund, S., J. Manyika, L.H. Segel, A. Dua, B. Hancock, S. Rutherford, and B. Macon. July 11, 2019. *The Future of Work in America*. McKinsey and company.

MacRumors Staff. August 18, 2022. "Apple Car." *MacRumors*. www.macrumors.com/roundup/apple-car/ (accessed May 5, 2022).

Maguire, J. September 13, 2019. "12 Examples of Artificial Intelligence: AI Powers Business." *Datamation*. www.datamation.com/artificial-intelligence/12-examples-of-artificial-intelligence-ai-powers-business/ (accessed April 25, 2022).

Maishman, E. July 24, 2022. "Chess Playing Robot Breaks Seven-Year-Old boy's Finger During Moscow Open." BBC.com. www.bbc.com/news/world-europe-62286017.amp.

Manyika, J., M. Chui, J. Bughin, R. Dobbs, P. Bisson, and A. Marrs. May 1, 2013. *Disruptive Technologies: Advances That Will Transform Life, Business, and the Global Economy*." Mckinsey.com.

Manyika, J., S. Lund, M. Chui, J. Bughin, J. Woetzel, P. Batra, R. Ko, and S. Sanghvi. November 28, 2017. *Jobs Lost, Jobs Gained: What the Future of Work Will Mean for Jobs, Skills, and Wages*, p. 21. Mckinsey.com. www.mckinsey.com/featured-insights/future-of-work/jobs-lost-jobs-gained-what-the-future-of-work-will-mean-for-jobs-skills-and-wages (accessed May 23, 2022).

Markoff, J. March 4, 2011. "Armies of Expensive Lawyers, Replaced by Cheaper Software." nytimes.com. www.nytimes.com/2011/03/05/science/05legal.html (accessed April 25, 2022).

Marr, B. 2020. *Tech Trends in Practice*, pp. 3–276. Wiley.

Marr, B. May 8, 2020. "5 Reasons Why Artificial Intelligence Really Is Going To Change Our World." *Forbes*. www.forbes.com/sites/bernardmarr/

2020/05/08/5-reasons-why-artificial-intelligence-really-is-going-to-change-our-world/?sh=3d982e9078b6 (accessed April 25, 2022).

Marsh, S. September 21, 2018. "Extreme Biohacking: The Tech Guru Who Spent $250,000 Trying to Live Forever." theguardian.com.

Marshall, A. July 25, 2021. "Trucks Move Past Cars on the Road to Autonomy." *Wired Magazine*. www.wired.com/story/trucks-move-past-cars-road-autonomy/ (accessed April 25, 2022).

Martin, N. March 19, 2021. "Mars Settlement Likely by 2050 Says Expert—But Not at Levels Predicted by Elon Musk." scitechdaily.com. https://scitechdaily.com/mars-settlement-likely-by-2050-says-expert-but-not-at-levels-predicted-by-elon-musk/ (accessed May 18, 2022).

Matthews, C. June 4, 2017. "Summers: Automation Is the Middle Class'[s] Worst Enemy." Axios.

Matthews, K. April 10, 2020. "5 Robots Now in Grocery Stores Show the Future of Retail." *Robotics Business Review*. www.roboticsbusinessreview.com/retail-hospitality/5-robots-grocery-stores-now/ (accessed April 25, 2022).

Max, D.T. March 21, 2011. "The Prince's Gambit." *The New Yorker*.

McDonald, M. August 6, 2013. "How Big Data Will Impact Employment and Human Resources." Venturebeat.com. https://venturebeat.com/2013/08/06/how-big-data-will-impact-employment-and-human-resources/ (accessed May 4, 2022).

McFarland, M. July 11, 2017. "Can Robots Solve Grandma's Loneliness?" *CNN*. https://money.cnn.com/2017/07/11/technology/culture/robot-senior-citizen/index.html (accessed April 25, 2022).

McKinsey Global Institute. December 2017. *Jobs Lost, Jobs Gained: Workforce Transitions in a Time of Automation*.

McLellan, C. 2019. *How Blockchain Will Disrupt Business*, p. 6. Tech Republic. www.techrepublic.com/resource-library/downloads/special-report/ (accessed April 26, 2022).

Meola, A. February 21, 2021. "Smart Farming in 2020: How IOT Sensors Are Creating a More Efficient Precision Agriculture Industry." *Business Insider*. https://www.businessinsider.com/smart-farming-iot-agriculture (accessed April 28, 2022).

Micron. n.d. "Insight: On the Road to Full Autonomy: Self-Driving Cars Will Rely on AI and Innovative Memory." *Micron Blog*. www.micron.com/insight/on-the-road-to-full-autonomy-self-driving-cars-will-rely-on-ai-and-innovative-memory (accessed April 25, 2022).

Miller, C.C. March 7, 2017. "How to Beat the Robots." *The New York Times*. www.nytimes.com/2017/03/07/upshot/how-to-beat-the-robots.html (accessed May 11, 2022).

Miller, K. June 4, 2020. "11 Data Science Careers Shaping Our Future." northeastern.edu. www.northeastern.edu/graduate/blog/data-science-careers-shaping-our-future/.

Mogensen, K. November 28, 2017. "Smart Society: How AI and Robots Will Change the World." *Scenario Magazine*.

Moore, G. 2014. *Crossing the Chasm*. Harper Business.

Morgan, L. April 29, 2021. "The Future of Data Scientist Jobs." techtarget.com. www.techtarget.com/searchenterpriseai/feature/The-future-of-data-science-jobs (accessed May 2, 2022).

Moutafis, R. July 13, 2021. "Is AI Coming for Your Job?" *Built In*. https://builtin .com/artificial-intelligence/ai-workers-jobs (accessed May 5, 2022).

Muro, M., J. Whiton, and R. Maxim. November 2019. "What Jobs Are Affected By AI? Better-Paid, Better-Educated Workers Face the Most Exposure." Brookings Institute. www.brookings.edu/research/what-jobs-are-affected-by-ai-better-paid-better-educated-workers-face-the-most-exposure/ (accessed April 25, 2022).

Najibi, A. October 24, 2020. "Racial Discrimination in Facial Recognition Technology." *Harvard University Science in the News*. https://sitn.hms.harvard .edu/flash/2020/racial-discrimination-in-face-recognition-technology/ (accessed April 25, 2022).

National Science Technology Council Committee on Technology (NSTC). 2016. *Preparing for the Future*, p. 16. obamawhitehouse.archives.gov.

Neufeld, D. October 25, 2021. "The Genomic Revolution: Why Investors Are Paying Attention." visualcapitalism.com. www.visualcapitalismcom/ the-genomic-revolution-why-investors-are-paying-attention/ (accessed May 2, 2022).

Ng, A. August 2, 2022. "What Your Car Knows About You." *Politico Digital Future Daily*. www.politico.com/newsletters/digital-future-daily (accessed August 2, 2022).

Novak, M. December 9, 2019. "U.S. Army Worries Humanity Is Biased Against Deadly Cyborg Soldiers Because of Movies Like 'Terminator'." Gizmodo .com.

O'Brien, E. April 13, 2020. "Market Playbook: 3 Examples of Robotics in Retail Transformation." *Robotics Business Review*. www.roboticsbusinessreview .com/opinion/what-will-become-of-the-unmanned-store/ (accessed April 25, 2022).

O'Connor, S. February 8, 2018. "Amazon Unpacked." *Financial Times*. www .ft.com/content/ed6a985c-70bd-11e2-85d0-00144feab49a (accessed April 25, 2022).

Oppenheimer, A. 2019. *The Robots Are Coming! The Future of Jobs in the Age of Automation*. Vintage Books.

Patch, M. January 23, 2020. "100 3D Printing Experts Predict the Future of 3D Printing in 2030." 3Dprintingindustry.com.

Pearce, M. July 26, 2021. "AI Deepfakes of Anthony Bourdain's Voice Are Only a Taste of What's Coming." *Los Angeles Times*.

Perelmuter, G. 2021. *Present Future: Business, Science, and the Deep Tech Revolution*, pp. 184–281. Fast Company Press.

Petrov, C. April 26, 2022a. "25+ Big Data Statistics 2022." techjury.net. https://techjury.net/blog/big-data-statistics/ (accessed May 2, 2022).

Petrov, C. April 26, 2022b. "49 Stunning Internet of Things Statistics 2022 [The Rise of IOT]." Techjury.net. http://techjury.net/blog/internet of things-statistics/ (accessed April 28, 2022).

Petrovic, K. November 5, 2020. "Picking Robots Address Agriculture's Labor Shortage Challenge." *Robotics Business Review*. www.roboticsbusinessreview.com/agriculture/picking-robots-address-agricultures-labor-shortage-challenge/ (accessed April 25, 2022).

Petrovic, K. June 22, 2021. "Farming With Driverless Tractors. Is It Possible?" *Robotics Business Review*. www.roboticsbusinessreview.com/opinion/farming-with-driverless-tractors-is-it-possible/ (accessed April 25, 2022).

Pickerel, K. August 9, 2021. "The U.S. Solar Industry Has a Chinese Problem." *Solar Power World*. www.solarpowerworldonline.com/2021/08/u-s-solar-china-polysilicon-battle/ (accessed April 25, 2022).

Piewa, K. October 16, 2019. "The Most Promising 3D Printed Organs Projects: 2021 Update." Sculpteo.com/blog. www.sculpteo.com/blog/2019/10/16/the-most-promising-3d-printed-organs-projects/ (accessed April 25, 2022).

Prabhune, M. January 22, 2021. "Top CRISPR Startup Companies Changing the Future of Biotech and Medicine." Synthego.com. www.synthego.com/blog/crispr-startup-companies (accessed May 5, 2022).

Purdy, M. April 6, 2022. "How the Metaverse Could Change Work." hbr.org. https://hbr.org/2022/04/how-the-metaverse-could-change-work (accessed June 24, 2022).

Raftery, B. April 1, 2022. "Meta, What? How the Metaverse and Augmented Reality Will Transform Entertainment." ew.com. https://ew.com/movies/the-future-metaverse-augmented-reality-entertainment/ (accessed June 28, 2022).

Rahman, T. March 19, 2020. "The Future of Nanotechnology." medium.com. https://medium.com/predict/the-future-of-nanotechnology-accddc9822fb (accessed May 8, 2022).

RBR Staff. March 10, 2020. "Built Robotics Partners With 400,000 Member Construction Union for Robotics Training Programs." *RBR*. www.roboticsbusinessreview.com/construction/built-robotics-partners-with-union-for-robotics-training-programs/ (accessed May 1, 2022).

Richards, J.W. 2018. *The Human Advantage: The Future of American Work in an Age of Smart Machines*. Crown Forum.

*Rise of the Humans 2: Practical Advice for Shaping a Workforce of Bots and Their Bosses*. 2017. kpmg.com.

*Rise of the Humans 3: The Integration of Digital and Human Labor*. 2018. kmpg .com.

Robb, D. January 29, 2022. "5 Trends in the Internet of Things (IOT) Job Market in 2022." *Datamation*. www.datamation.com/carrers/iot-job-trends (accessed April 27, 2022).

Roberts, D. October 21, 2020. "Geothermal Energy Is Poised for Big Breakout." *Vox*. www.vox.com/energy-and-environment/2020/10/21/21515461/renewable-energy-geothermal-egs-ags-supercritical (accessed April 28, 2022).

Robertson, D. July 20, 2022a. "A Comprehensive Vision of the Metaverse." *Politico Digital Future Daily*. www.politico.com/newsletters/digital-future-daily/2022/07/20/a-comprehensive-vision-of-the-metaverse-00046975.

Robertson, D. August 3, 2022b. "Good Paying (Virtual) Jobs." *Politico Digital Future Daily*. www.politico.com/newsletters/digital-future-daily/2022/08/03/good-paying-virtual-jobs-00049650 (accessed August 5, 2022).

Robitzski, D. January 14, 2020. "Paralyzed Man Runs Marathon in Robotic Exoskeleton." Futurism.com. https://futurism.com/neoscope/paralyzed-man-runs-marathon-robotic-exoskeleton (accessed May 2, 2022).

Robotiq. May 2020. *Collaborative Robot Buyer's Guide*. Version 8.1.

Roose, K. January 25, 2019. "The Hidden Automation Agenda of the Davos Elite." *New York Times*. www.nytimes.com/2019/01/25/technology/automation-davos-world-economic-forum.html (accessed April 25, 2022).

Roose, K. 2021. *Futureproof: 9 Rules for Humans in the Age of Automation*. Random House.

Ross, A. 2016. *The Industries of the Future*, p. 153. Simon & Schuster.

RTN Staff. October 17, 2019. "Restaurant Technology Spotlight: AUTEC Sushi Robots." *Restaurant Technology News*. https://restauranttechnologynews .com/2019/10/restaurant-technology-spotlight-autec-sushi-robots/ (accessed April 25, 2022).

Ruby, T. and N. Singh. January 24, 2017. "Realizing the Potential of CRISPR." McKinsey.com. www.mckinsey.com/industries/life-sciences/our-insights/realizing-the-potential-of-crispr (accessed May 5, 2022).

Sahoo, M. December 23, 2020. "Nanotechnology: Current Applications and Future Scope in Food." onlinelibrary.wiley.com. https://onlinelibrary.wiley .com/doi/full/10.1002/fft2.58 (accessed May 8, 2022).

Schatt, S. and M. Lobl. 2011. *Paint Your Career Green*. JIST.

Schindelheim, R. January 21, 2022. "The Green Economy: It's Bigger Than You Think and Growing Rapidly." Workingnation.com. https://workingnation .com/the-green-economy-its-bigger-than-you-think-and-growing-rapidly/.

Schreiber, N. October 28, 2021. "What Will It Take for Electric Vehicles to Create Jobs, Not Cut Them?" *The New York Times.* https://www.nytimes .com/2021/09/22/business/economy/electric-vehicles-jobs.html (accessed April 25, 2022).

Schroer, A. May 23, 2019. "AI and the Bottom Line: 15 Examples of Artificial Intelligence in Finance." *Built In.* Updated on July 11, 2021.

Schroer, A. March 11, 2022a. "How Artificial Intelligence in Business Is Changing the Way Companies Run and Employees Work." *Built In.* https:// builtin.com/artificial-intelligence/artificial-intelligence-in-business ( accessed April 25, 2022).

Schroer, A. March 16, 2022b. "12 Companies Turning AI Robots Into Real Life Wins." *Built In.* https://builtin.com/artificial-intelligence/robotics-ai-companies (accessed April 25, 2022).

Schroer, A. May 28, 2022c. "Artificial Intelligence in Cars Powers an AI Revolution in the Auto Industry." *Built In.*

Scott, K. April 3, 2020. "Ideas: Automation May Take Jobs." *Wired Magazine.*

Sharkey, N., A. van Wynsberghe, S. Robbins, and E. Hancock. 2017. "Our Sexual Future With Robots." *The Foundation for Responsible Robotics.*

Sharma, A. March 1, 2019. "Artificial Intelligence vs. Robotics: All the Facts You Need to Know." *Medium.* www.signitysolutions.com/blog/artificial-intelligence-vs-robotics-facts-need-know/.

Shaw, K. October 14, 2019. "Salad-Making Robot Earns Good Grades at Holy Cross." *Robotics Business Review.* www.roboticsbusinessreview.com/news/salad-making-robot-earns-good-grades-at-holy-cross/ (accessed April 25, 2022).

Shell, E.R. 2018. *The Job: Work and Its Future in a Time of Radical Change.* Penguin Random House.

Shewan, D. July 15, 2021. "10 of the Most Innovative Chatbots on the Web." *The Wordstream Blog.*

Simon, M. May 23, 2018. "This Robotic Pollinator Is Like a Huge Bee With Wheels and an Arm." wired.com. www.wired.com/story/robotic-pollinator/ (accessed April 25, 2022).

Simon, M. May 31, 2017. "Robots Wielding Water Knives Are the Future of Farming." *Wired Magazine.* www.wired.com/2017/05/robots-agriculture/ (accessed April 25, 2022).

Simon, M. June 1, 2021. "Peanut the Waiter Robot Is Proof That Your Job Is Safe." *Wired Magazine.* www.wired.com/story/peanut-the-waiter-robot-is-proof-that-your-job-is-safe/ (accessed April 25, 2022).

Simonite, T. June 3, 2021. "Don't End Up on This Artificial Intelligence Hall of Shame." *Wired Magazine.* www.wired.com/story/artificial-intelligence-hall-shame/ (accessed April 25, 2022).

Singh, D. October 16, 2020. "Retirement: Average Boomer's Savings Would Only Last Seven Years, Study Finds." yahoo.com. www.yahoo.com/video/boomers-savings-would-only-last-seven-years-in-ideal-retirement-160528666.html (accessed May 5, 2022).

Smith, A. and J. Anderson. August 6, 2014. *AI Robotics and the Future of Jobs.* Pew Research Center. www.pewresearch.org/internet/2014/08/06/future-of-jobs/ (accessed May 4, 2022).

Smith, A. and M. Anderson. October 4, 2017. "Americans' Attitudes Toward a Future in Which Robots and Computers Can Do Many Human Jobs." Pew Research Center. www.pewresearch.org/internet/2017/10/04/americans-attitudes-toward-a-future-in-which-robots-and-computers-can-do-many-human-jobs/ (accessed April 25, 2022).

Stahl, A. March 10, 2021. "How AI Will Impact the Future of Work and Life." *Forbes.* www.forbes.com/sites/ashleystahl/2021/03/10/how-ai-will-impact-the-future-of-work-and-life/?sh=5691adf079a3 (accessed April 25, 2022).

Stedman, C. February 23, 2022. "The Ultimate Guide to Big Data for Businesses." TechTarget.com. www.techtarget.com/searchdatamanagement/ (accessed May 2, 2022).

Steiner, C. 2012. *Automate This: How Algorithms Took Over Our Markets, Our Jobs, and the world.* Penguin.

Stone, P., R. Brooks, E. Brynjolfsson, R. Calo, O. Etzioni, G. Hager, J. Hirschberg, S. Kalyanakrishnan, E. Kamar, S. Kraus, K. Leyton-Brown, D. Parkes, W. Press, A. Saxenian, J. Shah, M. Tambe, and A. Teller. September 2016. *Artificial Intelligence and Life 2030: One Hundred Year Study on Artificial Intelligence,* pp. 11–101. Stanford.edu. https://ai100.stanford.edu (accessed May 1, 2022).

Sturgeon, J.M. February 7, 2017. "Finding Solutions to the Graying Caregiver Crisis." *Forbes.* www.forbes.com/sites/nextavenue/2017/02/07/finding-solutions-to-the-growing-caregiver-crisis/?sh=10a0a9ab2974 (accessed April 25, 2022).

Su, L.J. April 20, 2020. "What Will Become of the Unmanned Store?" *Robotics Business Review.* www.roboticsbusinessreview.com/opinion/what-will-become-of-the-unmanned-store/ (accessed April 25, 2022).

Susskind, R. and D. Susskind. 2015. *The Future of the Professions: How Technology Will Transform the Work of Human Experts.* Oxford University Press.

Swanson, C. February 2, 2015. "A Look Inside IBM Supercomputer Watson's New Cookbook." *Publishers Weekly.* www.publishersweekly.com/pw/by-topic/industry-news/cooking/article/65475-a-look-inside-chef-watson-s-new-book.html (accessed April 25, 2022).

Tangermann, V. December 12, 2019. "The Elderly in Japan Are Using Exoskeletons to Delay Retirement." futurism.com. https://futurism.com/neoscope/elderly-japan-exoskeletons (accessed May 2, 2022).

Tangermann, V. July 29, 2021. "Renewables Overtake Coal and Nuclear Power Generation in the U.S. Last Year: Clear Skies Ahead." Futurism.com. https://

futurism.com/the-byte/renewables-overtook-coal-and-nuclear-power-generation-us (accessed April 28, 2022).

Tayeb, Z. August 8, 2021. "NASA Wants Paid Volunteers to Spend a Year Living in a 3D Printed Martian Habitat in Texas, Where they Will Carry Out Spacewalks and Research Using VR Tech." Yahoonews.com. https://news.yahoo.com/nasa-wants-paid-volunteers-spend-101925164.html (accessed April 28, 2022).

Templeton, B. January 27, 2021. "AutoX Opens Real Robotaxi Service in China to the General Public." *Forbes.* www.forbes.com/sites/bradtempleton/2021/01/27/autox-opens-real-robotaxi-service-in-china-to-the-general-public/?sh=18ed032d5a6f (accessed May 22, 2022).

The Economist. June 23, 2016. "From Not Working to Neural Networking." *The Economist.*

The Economist. June 25, 2016. "Automation and Anxiety: Will Smarter Machines Cause Mass Unemployment?" *Special Report.*

The Economist. June 25, 2016. "March of the Machines: What History Tells Us About the Future of Artificial Intelligence—and How Society Should Respond." *Special Report.*

The Economist. June 25, 2016. "Re-educating Rita: Artificial Intelligence Will Have Implications for Policymakers in Education, Welfare and Geopolitics." *Special Report.*

The Economist. June 25, 2016. "The Return of the Machinery Question: After Many False Starts, Artificial Intelligence Has Taken Off. Will It Cause Mass Unemployment or Even Destroy Mankind? History Can Provide Some Helpful Clues, Says Tom Standage." *Special Report.* Economist.

The Economist. May 2018. *CMS, Artificial Intelligence and Robotics: From a Labour and Tax Perspective.*

Thiboudeau, P. January 16, 2014. "What STEM Shortage? Electrical Engineering Lost 35,000 Jobs Last Year." *Computerworld.*

Thomas, L. January 11, 2021. "Applications of Virtual Reality in Medicine." news-medical.net. www.news-medical.net/health/Applications-of-Virtual-Reality-in-Medicine.aspx (accessed April 28, 2022).

Thomas, M. January 3, 2022. "36 Robotics Companies on the Forefront on Innovation." *Built In.* https://builtin.com/robotics/robotics-companies-roundup (accessed April 25, 2022).

Thomas, M. February 18, 2022a. "The Future of Robots and Robotics." builtIn.com. https://builtin.com/robotics/future-robots-robotics (accessed April 25, 2022).

Thomas, M. March 28, 2022b. "33 Internet-of-Things (IOT) Companies You Should Know." *Built In.* https://builtin.com/internet-things/iot-internet-of-things-companies (accessed April 28, 2022).

Thomas, M. and B. Nordii. August 27, 2019. "Artificial Intelligence's Impact on the Future of Jobs." *Built In.*

Thomas, M. and B. Nordii. April 10, 2020. "Careers in Artificial Intelligence: A Look Into the Career Path of AI Professionals." *Built In.*

Thomas, M. and B. Nordii. December 9, 2021. "Is Artificial Intelligence a Good Career? These AI Professionals Think So." *Built In.*

Thomas, M. and B. Nordii. March 7, 2022. "15 Deep Learning Applications You Need to Know." *Built In.* https://builtin.com/artificial-intelligence/deep-learning-applications (accessed April 25, 2022).

Tomer, A., J.W. Kane, and C. George. February 23, 2021. "How Renewable Energy Jobs Can Uplift Fossil Fuel Communities and Remake Climate Politics." The Brookings Institute. www.brookings.edu/research/how-renewable-energy-jobs-can-uplift-fossil-fuel-communities-and-remake-climate-politics/ (accessed April 25, 2022).

Tong, C. February 18, 2020. "3D Printing Technology Helps Combat Ongoing Epidemic." *CFTN.* https://news.cgtn.com/news/2020-02-18/3D-printing-technology-helps-combat-ongoing-epidemic-ObLm59NsCQ/index.html (accessed April 26, 2022).

Trout, C. April 11, 2017. "RealDoll's First Sex Robot Took Me to the Uncanny Valley." *Engadget.*

Tudor, N. April 27, 2020. "5 Real-World Examples of How Brands Are Using Big Data." bornfight.com. www.bornfight.com/blog/7-real-world-examples-of-how-brands-are-using-big-data-analytics/ (accessed April 28, 2022).

Ulanoff, L. July 1, 2014. "Need to Write 5 Million Stories a Week? Robot Reporters to the Rescue." *Mashable.*

Venkat, K. March 4, 2020. "10 Examples of Artificial Intelligence in Manufacturing to Inspire Your Smart Factory." *Medium.* https://issuu.com/venkat34.k/docs/ai_in_manufacturing (accessed April 25, 2022).

Vuleta, B. April 28, 2021. "How Much Data Is Created Each Day? 27 Staggering Stats." seedscientific.com. https://seedscientific.com/how-much-data-is-created-every-day/ (accessed April 26, 2022).

Wadhwa, V. and A. Salkever. 2017. *The Driver in the Driverless Car: How Our Technology Choices Will Create the Future.* Berrett-Koehler Publishers.

Weinberg, N. August 28, 2019. "How SoftBank Robotics Builds Human Trust When Building Pepper." *Robotics Business Review.* www.roboticsbusinessreview.com/service/how-softbank-robotics-builds-human-trust-when-building-pepper/ (accessed April 25, 2022).

Werner, D. August 23, 2021. "Global Space Economy Swells in Spite of the Pandemic." spacenews.com. https://spacenews.com/space-report-2021-space-symposium/ (accessed May 18, 2022).

West, D.M. 2018. *The Future of Work: Robots, AI and Automation.* Brookings Institute Press.

White, S.K. April 25, 2022. "15 Best Data Science Boot Camps for Boosting Your Career." CIO.Com. www.cio.com/article/240719/10-boot-camps-to-kick-start-your-datascience-career.html.

Williams, M.S. May 27, 2021. "Life in 2050: A Glimpse at Space in the Future—Part I." interestingengineering.com. https://interestingengineering.com/life-in-2050-a-glimpse-at-space-in-the-future-part-i (accessed May 18, 2022).

Winkler, A. August 21, 2021. "Geothermal Energy Is on the Verge of a Big Breakthrough." *The Big Think.* https://bigthink.com/hard-science/geothermal-energy-verge-big-breakthrough/ (accessed April 28, 2022).

Winston, A. and H. Lovins. May 13, 2021. "Fossil Fuel Jobs Will Disappear, So Now What?" *MIT Sloan Management Review.* https://sloanreview.mit.edu/article/fossil-fuel-jobs-will-disappear-so-now-what/ (accessed April 28, 2022).

Wolf, M. October 7, 2021. "Called It: Just as We Predicted, Amazon Is Building a Smart Fridge." TheSpoon.tech. https://thespoon.tech/called-it-just-as-we-predicted-amazon-is-building-a-smart-fridge/ (accessed April 27, 2022).

Wooldridge, M. 2020. *A Brief History of Artificial Intelligence: What It Is, Where We Are, and Where We Are Going,* p. 156. Flatiron Books.

World Economic Forum. October 2020. *The Future of Jobs Report 2020,* p. 28. www.weforum.org/reports/the-future-of-jobs-report-2020/ (accessed April 25, 2022).

Wyatt, I.D. and D.E. Hecker. 2006. "Occupational Changes During the 20th Century." *Monthly Labor Review.* Bureau of Labor Statistics. www.bls.gov/opub/mlr/2006/03/art3full.pdf (accessed April 25, 2022).

Yonck, R. 2017. *Heart of the Machine: Our Future in a World of Artificial Emotional Intelligence,* pp. 81–82. Arcade Publishing.

Yamazaki, R., S. Nishio, H. Ishiguro, M. Nørskov, N. Ishiguro, and G. Balistreri. August 2014. "Acceptability of a Teleoperated Android by Senior Citizens in Danish Society." *International Journal of Social Robotics* 6, no. 3, pp. 429–442. www.proquest.com/openview/7ee3367beb853299ac2f3a30d63d0524/1?pq-origsite=gscholar&cbl=2043899 (accessed June 21, 2022).

Zimmer, C. July 26, 2021. "Scientists Finish the Human Genome at Last." nytimes.com. www.nytimes.com/2021/07/23/science/human-genome-complete.html (accessed May 2, 2022).

# About the Author

**Stan Schatt** has held senior management positions with some of the leading global technology research companies, including Forrester Research, Computer Intelligence, Giga Information Group, and ABI Research. He holds a PhD from the University of Southern California and an MBA from the American Graduate School of International Management (now Arizona State University). He has been cited for teaching excellence by USC, the University of Houston, and DeVry Institute of Technology. Schatt is the author of 50 books on a wide range of topics, including data communications, telecommunications, green technology, and data networks. He also has published fiction, including mysteries and science fiction.

# Index